Journey

Of

Intention

Life Made to Order

Derlene Hirtz

Thank you, Barb! God bless
you as you continue
on your journey.
Happy 90th
b-day! Love,
Derlene

First Edition, May 2016

Published by:
You.Empowered Services
P.O. Box 1547
St. Peters, MO 63376

Visit us at:
www.Youempoweredservices.com

ISBN 978-0-9974647-0-2

Cover by Hailey Kintz
Photo by Cyndi Palmer Photography

Journey of Intention is dedicated to all of you who seek to be the very best version of yourself. May you be empowered to seek, accept, and grow so that you may offer to others the entire person – spiritually, emotionally, and physically - you are called to be. May you seek the God within and witness God through all those put on your life path for your learning, growing, and serving. Ultimately, all the glory is to God.

Acknowledgements

A special thanks to my early mentors, Marya Pohlmeier and Rae Ann Keilty, both of whom saw in me what I failed to see in myself all those years ago. Thank you for your constant encouragement and acknowledgement. Thank you, Jim Wehmeier and Stacey O'Byrne, for standing along side me and challenging me as I learned to forgive, love, and accept the person of me. Ultimately, I can forgive, love and accept others without judgment through acceptance of myself. Funny how that works! Thank you, Shelly Cady, for walking up to me the first day of high school and introducing yourself; little could we have known all the life intersections that were ahead for us. Carol Wegeschiede, thank you for editing; I continue to learn! The many hours you spent editing are too numerous to count; please know I am forever grateful. To my family and friends, thank you for loving me. Most especially, my husband, Steve, for always standing along side me and encouraging my dreams. I am ultimately most appreciative to my God; for the gifts of my life, my struggles, my joys, and my tears – both of sadness and laughter. Every experience has led me to this moment of my amazing life journey.

"Give thanks to the Lord for His is good; his mercy endures forever." Psalm 107:1

Contents

Forward

Have you heard the saying "Life is a Journey"? If you have, how does it land for you? Is it cliché, does it have impact, or does it even have a meaning?

In today's busy world with the hustle and bustle of mere existence in a land of instant gratification, are we missing the true foundation of our time here on earth? Are we merely existing or are we truly living? Well, that is the question that gets to be answered.

Life is a journey. As a matter of fact, life is all about the journey. There is something innate in the way people choose to exist, to live. Some go through the motions, doing what they think is expected of them. For these people, life is just an existence. They may not feel like it or even realize that existing is really all that is happening. But if they were to step back, breathe, and observe their life, they would see that they get up, get the kids off to school, deal with traffic, go to work, come home, get the kids started on homework, do household chores, have dinner, maybe even watch TV, and then go to bed. Only to wake up the next day and rinse and repeat all over again. Others, barely show up for this game called life, maybe even do as little as possible. They may even have an excuse for everything and can justify and rationalize exactly why things are the way they are in their life at all times. While others find themselves stretched for time and completely stressed out and wake up one day wondering where the last 10 years have gone. Then there are those that thrive, embrace life to its fullest, carpe diem. What many fail to realize, and what Derlene Hirtz has mastered, is that need to connect to life, live to our fullest potential and embrace all there is to embrace out of every relationship, every lesson and every day.

If there is anything about your life that you wish could and would be different, then allow it to be so. Allow yourself to create your life. Live your life with intention. Get curious about the barriers that you have allowed into your existence, what purpose these barriers and limitations are serving, and how you can easily remove them. Then you can create, live, and have the life you have always wanted, know you deserve and were meant to live. No matter where you are in your life, no matter what your today looks like right now, you can create subtle little shifts that will impact massive change and shift your journey to one filled with intention versus settling for existence.

Once we embrace that we are the creator of our tomorrows, life becomes so much easier. We realize all of our experiences are really just compounded from choices we made from our yesterdays.

Derlene Hirtz is a proven empowerment and transformational specialist, and as I have witnessed firsthand, the very epitome of living life with intention that she writes of in this book. Some people are born with this talent, and some (like me) develop it over time when faced with dire straits. Derlene falls into both of these categories. Blessed with a natural ability to lead, she discovered the secrets to living life to its fullest. It is only natural that she, as one who thrives on "intention," would detail her journey and formulas for achievement for others. Likewise, it is only natural that I, as one dedicated to motivating and empowering others to succeed, would endorse this book. Derlene and I, while operating in different arenas, share a common truth: help others achieve their dreams and you will achieve yours.

So the question now dear reader is this: do you want to have, live and experience the life of your dreams? Maybe you are one of those people who want "more" but don't know how to connect to those in a position to help. Perhaps you are on top of your field and are suddenly aware that your good fortune is beginning to wane or possibly other areas of your life are suffering. Rather still, are you someone just realizing that you may possibly have an excuse for everything and are searching for a way to start you on the right path? If any of these are true, you are in luck. If you can remain focused on your journey to greatness, then Derlene Hirtz has provided a game plan, guide book, and testimonial to the path of overcoming setbacks and living your life by embracing a forever journey filled with intention.

Read on and live, love and aim high.

Stacey O'Byrne

Today I caught a glimpse of the woman you are becoming and thought I would share some thoughts with you. I just want to say, "You go girl!" There are very few people who really understand or know what you have put yourself through over the past few years. But I know and I just want to tell you that you are doing some awesome work! As you begin to walk more and more into My Light and leave the darkness behind, you will see everything changes; including discovering your passion and purpose for which you are here, making your dreams a reality, and understanding and embracing relationships. This is a revelation for you and it is exciting for Me to watch it all unfold. I see the energy you possess, the way you push yourself to know more, do more, and feel more. Yeah, feel more, that's new for you, too.

I really like the way you talk about the *dash*; you know, the line in between your birth year and your (future) death year. I love that the dash keeps getting thicker and thicker as you get older. Today I would call you happy. I see how you focus on authenticity. Living a life of joy, or what I call true freedom, is my greatest gift to you. You are happy; that comes from a joyful heart, a heart that looks to Me in all things, a heart that trusts that I am really at work here; you are the vessel bringing Me forth in your experience of life. All of these gifts offer you the truest freedom only found when you accept yourself for exactly who you are: created in My Image and My Love! I just want you to know that I am proud of your unwavering commitment to seek deep inside of yourself. It is not easy; no, quite the opposite, but worth every tear, struggle, fear, and anxious moment you have experienced.

Never forget you are made in My Image and My Likeness. One more thing, share your story with others so they will find hope and strength as they journey toward My Light as well.

Love ya! ~God.

This is the way I imagine God would be speaking to me if I were having a conversation with Him at this moment. It was not always easy for me though. I am the girl who always had a smile on her face so everyone accepted me as well-adjusted and happy. That is what I believed was expected, so that was what I delivered. It was not like I was always down in the dumps; actually the opposite. But there has always been this "nagging" pulling at me, begging me to address this part of my person. The "nagging" was like a voice always telling me there is more of "me" in who I am; I needed to quit holding it inside and share "me" with the world. For as long as I can remember, I would just push it back further and further back in my mind. Sometimes I even thought it disappeared entirely. Not so much. I was just much better sometimes than at others about ignoring it.

My time has come. I am answering the "nagging" that has long been in the depths of my mind, body and soul. I could not be more excited about my life and my future; which, by the way, with the grace of God, I am creating by the dreams I have and the choices I get to make.

I would like to share my journey, *Journey of Intention.* I call my journey one of intention because through the process of finding, accepting, and loving myself, I have made a conscious choice to be deliberate about every experience I have – good or bad – to learn, grow, accept, forgive and move on so that I can become the woman of God that I am called to be.

Each of the chapter titles in *Journey of Intention* begins with the word "An Offering." This is intentional on my part; that is all I can do: offer my experience, insight and wisdom. It is up to you to make a choice to discover who you are, what your passion and purpose is in your life, and create the life you choose to live.

God is always here with us; it is we who fail to recognize God at work through those who are put in our path. It is through these encounters with complete strangers, new and old friends, our family, and even those who hurt us that we are called to reflect, pray, learn the lessons and move forward in our life. It is not easy; we must do the work ourselves; no one can do that for us. However, we can accept those who cross our path as people sent, in some way, to impact our life. Our reaction to these friends and foes are what make all the difference in our future self.

One

An Offering ... Becoming Intentional

I started out with a spiritual desire to seek a deeper relationship with God; but it has become an awakening! I believed it would be easy to peer inside of myself and really get to know my true self. It would be insightful to figure out why I think like I think and act like I act. This way, I would at least understand my motives and thoughts behind my actions and be able to justify them; because, after all, that's just who I am and will always be. It is not like I set out to *change;* I was just looking for reasons for my thoughts and actions so I could excuse my behavior. Excuse myself for being sad, excuse myself for being lazy, excuse myself for taking so long to finish college; you get the point. I have always presented myself as a happy-go-lucky kind of girl. That should be good enough, right?

This is what I wanted everyone to believe; I was not prepared to take a real truthful look at who I was and definitely not about to peer into all my self-doubts and (dis)beliefs. It was much easier just *playing* Derlene. You know what I found out? It takes a lot of effort to be someone whom you think other people want you to be. Actually, it is exhausting: mentally, physically, emotionally, and for me, spiritually. I had grown weary.

I only began addressing the person of 'me' because I was called on the carpet by a friend. He asked me a question and I gave him the answer I thought he wanted to hear. I was asked point blank about why I was hiding what I really thought. It was as if he could see my mind trying to figure out what to say or my body trying to hide my surprise at his observation. "What are you talking about," I thought to myself. I knew, though. That "nagging" in my mind was really working overtime!

I admitted, in that moment as well as my desperation to squelch that constant "nagging" found deep inside my heart and soul, that it was time for the true me to emerge; whoever that might be. I had grown weary of the on-going sense of helplessness and hopelessness. I began to listen to the people God put in my path to help and support me. I had reached moments where I was so anxious I would hide from my husband, Steve, my children, my friends and even my family that was visiting from out of town.

Steve has always worked out of town and when he was home, I took to hiding away in some other part of the house or working long hours so there was no opportunity to get cornered and questioned. He knew I was struggling but what should he say to me? I would only snap back if questioned anyway.

I would talk to my son and daughter daily on the phone, staying on just long enough to make sure they were okay. When I hung up, I would tell myself they were just talking to me out of obligation; no real conversation had taken place. I would rationalize, they didn't "get" me, and they were not interested in the same things as me. I would make all kinds of excuses that centered on them, not me. After all, I was just fine and dandy.

It was easy to pretend to be happy around friends. We were only together a couple of hours a month at the most. I can do anything for a couple of hours, especially if I had a glass or two of wine. I can remember standing at a picnic with hundreds of people there, many of whom I knew, and feeling so alone. Friends would come up and talk and I would act all cheerful. They would walk away and I would think to myself,

"See, you can fool them!" As soon as they walked away, I would immediately start the emotional "yelling" at myself. I would remind myself that I was blessed with so many friends. In the next breath ask myself what was wrong with me? How come I didn't "feel" happy? I should be happy, what on earth did I have to feel sad about? I cannot even count how many times I repeated this cycle. I never could come to any revelation with those questions.

My family lives out of town so the phone calls were disguised as "all is well here!" I just played along with what I believed were the expectations of the conversations. It was brilliant and worked great. Yeah, that was sarcastic!

As months passed after my friend's query, the emotional intensity kept increasing; I knew I was no longer going to be able to live this way. Although, knowing is one thing, doing is another. It was getting more and more difficult to hide. On the other hand, I did not dare let anyone else in on the constant panic and deep longing inside my soul to feel complete, whole and comfortable in my own skin.

Timing is everything. Actually, timing is all God's, and the time for me to leave behind the "junk in my trunk" had finally come. When my friend challenged me about what I was really thinking and what I truly believed about myself, I knew he was speaking out of concern. I am sure there have been other people in my life who have expressed worry or questioned me; but the timing was not right for me to hear them. In that moment I genuinely decided to make a commitment to explore my values and beliefs and to intentionally set out to discover why I was put on this earth and what plans God has for me. For the first time, I wanted to really dream. I wanted to create real meaningful goals for myself that would make my life-dash

I spoke about earlier grow thicker by the month, week, and even day.

I have grown to realize every experience, thought, action, and emotion in my life is an opportunity to recognize that I am called to make a choice: I can run and hide or I can see the experience as a gift. It does not matter if I planned on receiving the gift or not; it is mine to graciously accept. I then make my next choice; unwrap the treasure or just let set it on a shelf (of my mind) somewhere. If I unwrap it, I will be called to reflect, learn, and grow through the potentially life-changing experience. The other choice I have is to leave it on the shelf, allowing it to collect dust, perhaps occasionally be curious about what is in it but then dismiss it as something I probably do not need or want for that matter.

I once read a story about a young man graduating from college. His dad was very wealthy and could pretty much afford anything as a gift for his son. The boy had his eye on a sports car and told his dad about how much he would love to have it as a graduation present.

Graduation day came and the father presented him with a gift. Upon opening it and discovering it was a Bible, the son became very angry and stomped out. It was the last time he saw his father.

Many years later and after finding his own success, the son decided his father was getting old and he should really go to see him. Before he could make the arrangements, his father died, leaving all his possessions to the son. When going through his father's possessions, he came across the Bible his father had given him all those years before. This time he took it out of the case and started looking at it. It was beautiful! As he began to turn the pages something fell from the back of the

Bible. It was keys to the car that his father had purchased for him all those years ago in honor of his college graduation.

The son did not receive the gift that he wanted, or so he thought. It was there all along. In his anger or disappointment, he did not look any deeper to discover the treasure that was his for the taking.

Reading this reflection, I am curious as to how his life would have been altered had he been a gracious receiver. Perhaps on the other hand, the many lessons he was called to learn would not have occurred had he completely unwrapped his gift.

I used to think I would one day write a book about friendships I have been blessed to have throughout my life. I remain fascinated by how different each personal relationship is nurtured and so unique from other friendships. How can I feel so close to a friend I just met? Isn't it exciting to run into a friend I have not seen in years, yet it was just like yesterday? Why do some friendships just die out?

That very thought was on my mind when I began to write this book. As I was brainstorming and then writing, the words and stories just never felt right to me. During these many months as I have been reflecting and writing, my search deep within me was, and is, continually discovering new insight to my thoughts, actions and reactions as well. This has all been a realization to help me truly become aware of myself and accept me...for me.

As it turned out, the yearning desire to write about friendships was actually a misunderstanding on my part. I came to appreciate I was not so much fascinated by the friendships in and of themselves; I was actually seeking friendship within myself. If I kept myself busy with relationships whether it was offering advice, going out for dinner, shopping together or just listening to what is on their mind, then I would be safe from focusing on my inner self. Besides, I am a person of service; I need to help where and when I am needed. It is so much "safer" to help someone out rather than to address myself.

And so the next chapter of my life journey begins. The difference between yesterday and today is I am being very intentional in how I accept my daily life. I no longer look at even the simplest day to be repetitive or boring. I am living my dash, living the life gifted to me by God.

As my new journey began to unfold, I set out to finally answer the voice inside of my unconscious mind. Do what? Remember what? Say what? Feel what? Be what? All of those questions have been nagging inside of my soul for almost as long as I can remember. As I prepare for the journey ahead I think of Dr. Seuss: "Oh the places you will go!" I have to get ready for the ride of my life. I realize I am about to journey on an unknown path that goes through unlit tunnels of complete darkness where I will have to trust that my Engineer knows exactly what He is doing and that I will reach my destination completely intact.

I have previously allowed fear to be one of the biggest factors in my decision making. No more. Instead, I have become excited about what may be in that unlit tunnel. It is like I am carrying a backpack full of tools, emotions, and thoughts that either help me or hold me back. By learning to toss away what does not aid me and put in more of what does, I know I am on my path to true freedom. I will continue to grow into my full potential as a woman of God. I want to do this for me, to prove to myself that I have moved past those constant feelings of darkness and created an amazing life for myself.

Just as important as showing myself, I want to show my God how grateful I am by living my life rooted in authentic happiness and love; a life that glorifies Him through who I am.

I do not want to miss a gift from God; I am going to open up my gifts and peer inside. I know I will make the choice to decide how it serves me. Maybe it doesn't serve me and I move on to the next moment. However, there is a wonderful chance it contains an experience that is life changing. One thing I know for certain: it can only happen if I am willing to be open to any and all gifts that are entrusted to me. I do not get to pick and choose; no, that would be too easy. Besides, where is the adventure in that?

I have grown to accept and embrace every gift God offers me. I no longer view my life as "woe is me" or "I am so lucky." Luck has no place in my life. What I now embrace is that I am blessed beyond all measure! I have a family that loves me, friends that encourage me, and a career that supports my mission to continually seek to be a better and better version of myself. As I acknowledge and learn from the insight, the world around me is greatly affected as well. I think that is pretty awesome.

Give thanks to the LORD, for he is good; his love endures forever. Psalm 107:1

Wisdom has shown me there will be times that I am so consumed by the powerful sunshine that is love; it will be easy to offer thanks to God. I love imagining the feeling of standing on the top of a high mountain: wind blowing ever so slightly; surrounded by creation; arms stretched out; head tilted back with my body feeling the effects of the healing sun; remaining so quiet and still that I can take in all the holy power that comes from realizing I am the vessel of a loving God that tells me I am perfectly made in the image and likeness of Him. And that is just perfect.

I am also aware there will be days in between that offer their fair share of gloom, little light and subtle messages trying to convince me of untruths. It is at these moments I am called to pay attention and trust in God's enduring love. It is here where I am so tempted to shelf the gift. Oh but I must not!

Those are the moments that call me to move forward in my life – growth opportunities that are mine for the taking. Not to soak in self-doubt, but to recognize this is where courage lies and strength is to be built; moments God designed for me personally. Not for me to live in self-pity, make excuses or look to others to dig me out. In fact, those moments are given to me so that I can embrace who I am and do whatever work is necessary. Perhaps the growth is in forgiving someone who has hurt me or maybe it is the humbling moment of asking someone I have hurt for forgiveness. Perhaps the gift lies in my ability to admit or face up to choices I have made or does the gift lie in simply discovering another layer of myself that I have not previously met. We all have different reasons we are called to grow and learn. What I do know is that these are the moments I choose to become intentional on my journey of this amazing gift called life and seek to discover the person who is me.

The best news of all is that you only need to have the desire. Trust that people who will help you along on your self-discovery will simply show up at the right place at the right time. You just need to pay attention! Listen when you hear a voice that talks to your heart; you may not always want to hear what is being said; however, there is almost certainly a learning that you will need to take with you as you move forward on the next step that awaits you.

One of those "learnable" moments was when my girlfriend, Sonja, was in town visiting some high school friends and staying in my home. As I was taking her back to the airport, we passed a man that I had noticed for some time living out of his car in one of the commuter parking lots right off the highway. I flippantly pointed him out as we drove past. He had water jugs on top of his roof, what looked like his clothes being used as window coverings, and the car itself looked as if it had been through a number of very tough years. It certainly did not look like it actually was drivable!

I dropped Sonja off and headed back to get to church not giving the homeless man a second thought. Church that day included the Gospel reading from St. Luke where Jesus is asked, "Who is my neighbor?" Talk about an "aha" moment on my path at just the right time! That very instant the homeless man and my attitude towards him popped into my mind. A very humbling moment when I accepted he was no longer a stranger to me; in that instant he became my neighbor. The next question I asked myself was, "How do I help my new neighbor?" It sure didn't look like he had much of anything. I felt it was my responsibility to do something; I felt guilty for being so uncaring towards his obvious situation.

I enlisted the help of a friend who went shopping with me and we purchased all sorts of personal hygiene and food items such as pop tarts, a fresh sandwich, and peanut butter. I was feeling really good about serving my neighbor!

We finished our shopping and drove to the parking lot. I was very surprised by what happened next; the homeless man, my new neighbor, was no longer there! I could hardly believe my eyes. Where could he have gone? His car didn't even look like the engine would turn over.

We laughed at the irony of the whole event. Me, trying to do a good deed; my friend graciously agreeing to go along with me; and the man elsewhere in his car, which by the way, obviously ran. It was pretty funny. As we headed back home, I agreed to leave everything in my car and promised not to approach him alone; even though he was my neighbor, I did not actually *know* him.

Oh the lessons I learned, even in the moments when I believed I was doing right and good for my neighbor. Although I was well intended, I acted on what I believed the man needed; in reality, when we finally caught him on the parking lot some days later, his car was not only his home, it was also his storage. He said he would not keep anything that he did not need or could not use. My recollection is that he kept the peanut butter and hand sanitizer. Had I stopped and asked him what it was he needed prior to going shopping, my money and time would have been better spent; he sure could have used some new t-shirts. It was quite humbling.

The homeless man adventure was just getting me started for the day. I never could have imagined the holy encounter that lay ahead. Dropping off my friend, I decided to get a quick bike ride in before the sun set. Stopping to get gas, I noticed an old Mustang convertible next to me. It looked to be about as old as the one I drove as a kid, only this was a convertible. I asked the man who was pumping gas if I could take a peek – it was in such perfect condition and memories of my high school days were flowing in my mind. I noticed he had a big baseball bag in the back of his seat. He told me he was a coach for some young boys. As he began explaining about his reasons for coaching, the conversation turned much more somber.

His son, who was in high school at the time, was passionate about baseball. It was a bond between father and son; much similar to my own son and his dad. As he continued sharing the story, he explained his son had died in a freak accident years before. Tears welled up in his eyes and he shared some wonderful memories about his son. There is even a baseball diamond named in his honor and memory. He talked about how he only survived this great tragedy because he and his wife turned to their faith in God to get them through those moments of unbearable grief; how everyday they still grieve but have a wonderful community that supports and loves them.

At some point in the conversation, we looked at each other and realized how surreal this time between two complete strangers was. Even as I write about this story - that dreamlike feeling of entering into a very intimate conversation, sharing stories about our families, feeling like time was standing still, and completely trusting our story with a stranger - all of this had to be designed by a God who knew what we needed in that moment.

The difference between this moment and thousands of others like it was that both of us were open to the experience of encountering the God within. We mostly shared about how we do our best to allow God to be the guiding force in our lives and the strength that comes from those times when we completely surrender ourselves to Him. This unshakable trust is what gets his family through their daily lives and past those moments that still hurt so deeply. Coaching is one of the most effective ways he has been able to mourn his son while keeping his spirit alive.

Our gas tanks were obviously filled an hour and a half later, and we each went our separate ways promising to keep each other in prayer. Mustang man, as I affectionately call him, could have never known how powerful that time was for me. I was struggling with figuring out so much of my life; I realized in that conversation I could and would open myself to all that God asks of me. My resolve to walk further and further away from those dark places in my mind was even more solidified in that hour and a half.

By this time, it was too late for the bike ride; I headed home and reflected on the many lessons learned in only one day. I was called to my prejudice of the homeless man through the Gospel at church, and let's be honest, my ignorance as well! I would not be writing this story today if I had not asked to see Mustang Man's car. To commune with God in that sacred moment of sharing his story and mourning the loss of his son are among some of the holiest moments of my life. God reminds us how blessed we are through the story of His other sons and daughters.

People are placed in our lives for very particular reasons; I try not to let those reasons go unnoticed on my journey. That is what I mean by intentional. I look for the wisdom in each "gift" I receive; including and especially the ones I really do not want to accept or address. However, these two stories have been life altering for me in many ways. I have grown in my understanding and acceptance of my neighbor and shared compassion and grief with a total stranger which resulted in my stronger commitment to continuing my intentional journey. Funny, how with God, there are no accidents.

As I began listening to the voice inside my head, my life began moving and shifting with wonderful and unexpected opportunities of discovery. Name the voice; whatever it is that you feel is right for you: God, Spirit, higher power, guardian angel, or unconscious mind. For me, God has been my Creator from the moment of my birth. My faith is the heart beat of my life; with every breath I take, I thank God for allowing me this opportunity to share my story with the hope that the person reading it can identify with its honesty and authenticity. It is my prayer you will begin living your life with great intention, welcome those ongoing thoughts that swirl around in your mind with great curiosity, and begin learning and growing in ways that leave you amazed and wanting to awaken even more the beautiful person of you. We are each given opportunities every day to grow into a better version of ourselves. How cool is that!

I seek to be a woman of intention in every moment I am granted...how about you? Are you ready to begin your *Journey of Intention?*

Two

An Offering ... Messengers

We are all messengers. I am. You are. Friend and foe alike are all messengers. We are sent to be envoys to and for each other: to serve one another, and then in those times of need, to accept the help and love of those who serve us. The difference between other messengers and me is that I am choosing to share my message, my story, with you. I choose to share because I am convinced that I can encourage you to become a seeker – seeking to accept the marvelous person of you and then setting out to discover the many wonderful gifts you have been given; only to share them with others, who will in turn, seek change and then share their gifts. The circle will always continue long after we have reached the end and the time has come to add a date to the other end of our dash. All of this because we made a choice to share our love with the world.

Messengers, like friendships, are sent to enter our life, either for a fleeting moment, quick in and out in a short time, or for a lifetime of engagement. We have had messengers throughout history that changed the course for the world, nation, and for us personally. Imagine if Moses had refused to be a messenger for God. Okay, maybe he did at first, but he did eventually jump on board! God trusted Moses and in doing so gave us the Ten Commandments and led an entire nation to freedom. Here was a man who as a baby, who was sent in a basket down the river, who killed another man, who stuttered so badly he couldn't talk in public, and who initially did not want to obey God. Look what he did for those who believe. All I can say is God has a lot of confidence in His messengers!

Martin Luther King was a great messenger of his time. He worked tirelessly for non-violence as a means to peace. Like

Christ, he openly lived what he professed: treat all people with dignity and with the respect all humanity deserves. It would have been very easy for Dr. King to become a doctor or lawyer; he had the means and was brilliant. Had Martin Luther King chosen to stay silent and stand on the sidelines, he might have lived a longer life; but, no doubt, he would have died a man knowing he never reached his full potential. Dr. King responded to the nudge from God. I am in awe of his conviction and courage in delivering the message that would eventually cost him his life.

Mother Theresa is another amazing example of delivering her message to the entire world. The no nonsense founder of the Sisters of Charity did not have any intention of becoming famous. Seeing the destitute and dying prompted her into action. She embraced her role as a woman who loved all humanity. She delivered her message of love to the poor, the sick, and the dying. She had witnessed her mother delivering messages of hope while feeding the community's hungry in her own home. It was only natural for Mother Teresa to say yes when she felt called to care for the people of Calcutta. With compassion and love, Mother Theresa lived among the poorest of the poor on earth. She loved them literally into their death. For me, her most powerful message was to not let pain and suffering isolate you; through pain and suffering all humanity stands united. What a message, what a blessing to humanity this messenger was and even no longer alive, still is for us today.

I wonder if Moses, Dr. King, and Mother Theresa ever wondered why they were chosen to be messengers. I wonder if they ever thought they couldn't possibly be the deliverer because they were not educated, didn't speak well in front of others, or if they believed there were many others who could be more effective or eloquent in the written word. Each of these courageous people took a huge leap of faith by answering the nudge and embracing their role as messenger. They were very much aware there would be those who heard and would reject them; that did not deter them. They accepted their call and delivered messages of peace, freedom, and love for all humanity. What role models!

Writing my story, I have asked myself those same questions. Why do I feel called to share my story? I am no one special; I certainly am no Moses, Mother Teresa or Dr. King! I am not eloquent in my speech nor do I have a PhD. My story is not really that unique from that of thousands of others. Why do I have to be the one to lay my feelings and emotions on the table? And then I think, if not me, then who? That question was asked over and over again by my friend and coach, Stacey. When I couldn't tell her the "who" answer, I realized it was me. So I accept this gift and share what I have learned in my search and understanding of my destiny. As a matter of fact, I believe *Journey of Intention* is essential to my destiny. It is my prayer that one person will read this, feel the nudge and begin seeking his or her personal journey of intention.

Do not conform yourselves to this age but be transformed by the renewal of your mind, that you may discern what is the will of God, what is good and pleasing and perfect. Romans 12:2

It is very difficult to actually hear, ingest, change and live anew a message that can disrupt the easy fashion we call our daily life. It is actually easier to tell ourselves that all is fine; life is good. We have a roof over our head, people who love us, a good job, and on and on goes the list of excuses. We have these thoughts or feelings of being called to a new journey or a nagging that is not in line with whom or what we want to be.

Perhaps we believe we should be this person because our family expects it. We feel guilty because, for all intent purposes, we have a great life. But why then, does the nagging feeling or thoughts keep showing up? Or why do we refuse to forgive ourselves, or someone that has hurt us?

We all struggle at some point in our life. It shows up at different times given different circumstances and previous experiences. If we do not face our emotions and feelings, we continue to live in a world that we know is not complete. We can make excuses for everything that goes wrong in our life. We can even make excuses for the good in our life. Have you ever given someone a complement or said she did a good job and she made an excuse as to why?

It is human nature to get off track; we are made in His image and likeness – we are not God. So we mess up. I have made mistakes inadvertently; other times I knew the mistakes were wrong when I made them; they were moments of weakness that I choose to give in to. There were times when it is just easier.

The next choice is what makes all the difference in our world. If we admit to our sinfulness, deal with and forgive it, we will move forward. Sometimes, we get stuck in making excuses for our behavior. If I have said it one time, I have said it hundreds, "I just cannot forgive myself." It is as if we are treading water to stay afloat. Our legs are kicking furiously in the water, our arms moving back and forth. We can feel the burn, the anxiety, can't we? We get tired. Maybe we are calling for help; perhaps, we still believe we can get to the shore by ourselves. We get exhausted and we begin to sink.

Is it not the same scenario we deal with in our heart? We get ourselves into a situation where we make a choice. In our humanism, and for whatever reason, this choice is the one that brings darkness, not light. Our mind is on overdrive; we try to rationalize. We make excuses. Finally, since we hold ourselves up to such impossible standards, we begin to sink. We fall into a darkness that we begin to embrace and claim as our life. Living a life full of regret will never allow us to move forward toward the essences of our true selves. We know this is so; but sometimes the darkness is our comfort zone; it is what we have come to accept and so we call it living.

Throughout my life God has sent me messengers. Their role would be that of a mentor, protector or advisor. Many times I listened but did not truly hear. I lived the "in one ear and out the other" mentality. However, I reached a point in which I felt like there was no other choice; I became increasingly desperate, and finally, I paid attention. It was my time to become fully engaged in life once again, or in some ways, the first time ever.

God's timing was (as always) impeccable. People showed up and I began actually listening to them. I suppose there have been others along the way. I either could not or would not hear them. I wouldn't say that I jumped right on board with great enthusiasm as they began appearing, perhaps even to the contrary. However, my messengers never gave up on me. Slowly, layer upon layer of confusion, sadness, even hopelessness faded away as I began embracing a message rooted in love and kindness that eventually led me to move forward. I began to see and hear many truths in these messages. I learned how to move away from living in excuses and complaints; that alone is one of the great gifts hand delivered by my messengers. My couriers came in different ages and both genders. I had to learn to trust; I had to discern if this friend was helping me, and I had to make a choice to move from the place I had been stuck in for many years, or not. Ultimately, the choice is always mine.

I had been feeling like I did not belong in my community, in my marriage, in my work, and in my friendships for so long that on some days, I was willing to accept that as my life: hopeless. I would occasionally allow the true feisty me to show herself and I would refuse to be so accepting of my dark, lonely thoughts, only to once again feel hopeless. I would start condemning myself with my own words: you have a great life so what's your problem; you have everything you want, why are you not satisfied; you have an amazing family, why do you think they don't love you, you are selfish, you are spoiled, and I could go on. Down my little dark path I would go. I spent many nights tearing myself apart and holding myself to such a high standard that it was impossible to ever live up to how perfect I expected me to be. I realize that now. My survival technique was to blame anyone and everyone for my state of despair.

I would talk to my spiritual director about these feelings. She was the only person who really knew at that time that I was struggling, feeling so alone and so helpless. We would scrape away little bits of what was going on inside of me time and time again. I revisited them many times, over and over. I looked so forward to going to her and receiving her counsel (still do as a matter of fact). This was the beginning of my *Journey of Intention;* I just didn't know it as this yet.

To the outside world I appeared very happy, comfortable and engaged in life. This was true to some extent; it is not like I was always in an obvious constant struggle. The way I can explain how I felt was there was this consistent nagging in my head. It was always there, even when I was smiling, laughing, and what I deemed as "living." Occasionally, I would think, "What is going on?"

I reached the point where I was living everyday aimlessly trying to figure out why I always felt so sad, alone, and hopeless. I didn't understand why I was on such an emotional roller coaster; I just knew that I felt desperate most of the time. Yet, if you would have seen me at work or out and about town, I would have had a smile on my face and "acting" as if I were the happiest person on earth. When in reality, I wanted to run away from my life. How could I, who had a fabulous life with lots of friends, a beautiful home, a husband who loved and supported me and a family who thought I was on top of it all, feel so distracted, feel so disjointed and feel so alone?

A friend was sharing with me about her child who was experiencing an unfathomable amount of emotional pain. Kids are supposed to go to school and feel safe. They should learn and be happy. That was not happening at the school; and her child was suffering so much that the school was no longer an option for him to attend. The child explained that it was as if there were two people inside of his body: one part of him was who he showed to the world and the other one just wanted to yell, scream and cry, "Can't anybody see how I really feel?"

I thought to myself, "I know this feeling, I have lived it for many years." I could empathize with the young person's yearning for all the pain and sadness to just go away. And then, I felt guilty for feeling the way I did. All the people in my life would shake their head in disbelief that I was on such a dark journey (and probably will if they read this). I thought I was that good at disguising what was constantly swirling around in my head.

One of my messengers came in the most surprising time of my life. Okay, maybe not so surprising if I am really honest. God provides when necessity warrants.

God places people in our lives at just the right time for a particular purpose. Through many different paths, Jim kept crossing over into my life. First he was involved in business with my sister, then he was interested in a mission trip I was going on, and lastly he joined a youth group team at my invitation. It was as if God was not going to let what he had to bring into my life pass me by. It is surreal when I think about how many times our lives crisscrossed in a very short amount of time.

As I write this I am amazed at God's constant interference into my self-pity! I was so consumed in my reasons for not embracing the potential for my life that I had become stuck in the day-to-day things I did to survive: get up, have coffee, beg God for some kind of relief, go into the world with my happy smile, come home and live the night in a silent declining spiral. I could not or would not talk to Steve because I was afraid I would say something that he would not understand or react in a way I couldn't emotionally handle. I would come up with reasons for avoiding going home. We all have our excuses for why we cannot get out of that deep, dark hole we get into. Jim was not going to allow me to stay there.

I know now that you cannot see in someone else that which doesn't exist in you. (You may want to read that again.) Jim saw similarities in his own journey and pretty much could call me on the carpet about what I was thinking. Had he always been the person he is today, he would have been unable to detect the rote answers and fake smiles that I always presented. There were similarities in my responses he once recognized in himself. I will always be thankful he remained completely present to answer any call that I made in those desperate moments when I was trying to cope and get through to the next day, sometimes even the next moment. Those conversations were lifesavers as well as life changers for me.

I began trusting. For the first time in a long time, I would say to Jim what I was really feeling as opposed to replying in a response that was safe. I figured he would never talk to me again with my honest answers and truthful feelings. After all, that is what I usually did when I got into a bind – run, hide or escape either physically or emotionally – I expected Jim to do the same. However, he was not about to let me off the hook that easily. Instead, he brought to my attention that it was the first time I had ever really made myself vulnerable. I have to admit, when I heard that word in reference to me, I was shocked. Me, vulnerable? Oh no, I was stronger than the weakness of being vulnerable! I thought to be vulnerable was to allow someone to take advantage of me. I was not going to be put in a position where I was going to be seen as weak. No way; besides, he was supposed to run in the other direction! I wanted to get back to my pity party! I have never allowed myself to be vulnerable; that was an accident, I didn't mean for that to happen! Now what?

There was that part of me that was hoping Jim would never talk to me again. After all, he was asking me questions that I did not want to answer and bringing to my attention things that made me truly face myself and deal with me! He kept telling me I was allowing thoughts into my mind; I needed to change the way I was thinking. I had to stop thinking like I was a failure and stop being so hard on myself. I kept saying I just did not understand why I felt like this. I was insistent. I had to have an answer to that question – why did I feel like this?

At first I didn't know what Jim meant when he would say that I had control of what I allowed in my head. He would say, "You can't control the first thought because it is impulse but what you can control is the second thought and what the second thought feeds." I was so tired of thoughts about my imperfections, choices I regretted, and how I viewed my life; I just wanted to not think anymore. I wanted to run, anywhere, just run. But where you go you follow, right? And follow I did.

The first time I heard where you go, you follow, I didn't get it. I thought if I would change my environment, I would see life differently. It was like if I lived in the mountain and moved to the desert, my attitudes, thoughts, and actions would all change in an instant. Then, I had an "aha" moment. It didn't matter if I stayed where I was or ran away to the mountains, my thoughts, feelings, emotions, all of it, was going right along with me. I might as well face them and learn from them. Otherwise, I would remain stuck in this place which only offered me misery. The way I saw it, those were the choices that were available.

One of the most difficult times I faced during this "growth spurt" was during a visit from my parents at Christmas. I was excited they were coming yet regretting it all in the same breath. I did not understand how I could be so excited in one moment and dreading their visit in the next; that was my roller coaster I was traveling. I was afraid they would see what a mess I was and then they would be so worried; and I reasoned, what could they do anyway? Besides, I knew I would not allow any vulnerability to be seen.

I was so distraught at one point I had to go to the bathroom and call Jim. Since he was only one of two persons I had been confiding in, I knew he would help me rationalize my anxiety. I just could not do it on my own. Realizing that I needed his help, I would then start berating myself asking what was wrong with me that I could not handle these little situations by myself. As they days went on, the cycle would repeat itself over and over again.

My two friends kept encouraging me to quit thinking I wasn't good enough and to stop always thinking that no one loved me. Obviously my parents love me, they traveled from Texas in the winter for heaven's sake! Having regained my composure, I hung up, put a smile on my face and went out to the living room. Just like always.

I made an excuse that I needed to workout at the gym. I grabbed my gym clothes and headed out into the cold. We had a fresh ice storm that came through our town. It did not occur to me in that moment perhaps I should not be out driving in the ice.

As I was traveling down the road, I noticed the fresh ice sitting on the branches of the bare trees and sparkling like diamonds. It was one of the most beautiful scenes in nature I have ever laid my eyes on. The little crystals mimicked diamonds sparkling as the sun bounced from limb to limb. In that moment, I decided to stop in the middle of the road, hold my phone up and snap a few pictures to remind me of the beauty of God's creation. As I was reflecting, the moment seemed almost surreal. Here I was in the middle of feeling so sorry for myself and the most beautiful picture of nature was right in front of me. It snapped me out of my latest pity party.

That is when I received the gift! I literally held up my phone, pointed it in the direction of the trees, and clicked away. I was clicking really fast because I had stopped in the middle of the road and didn't want anyone to hit me. I glanced down at the pictures and all I could see was a bright light. I wondered what that was because I was searching for my little crystals sitting on the branches. I pulled over at the first opportunity. This is one of five pictures I took:

Every one of the pictures had a cross in it! I was completely overwhelmed. I couldn't stop looking at them. I knew. I just knew in that moment that God was sending me a message of hope and love. Once again God was saying, "I got this, you only need to trust me." A deep heavy sigh followed. I began understanding I was being called to this dark space in my beautiful life because I needed to grow and move from where I had been stuck for so long.

The love, the hope, the trust, all of which I had been searching for so long was in that picture. To this day these pictures remain among my greatest treasures. I knew this was my own private gift from my God telling me to trust in my journey. Once again, without a doubt, I would not be writing this story if I had not been paying attention to the messages and messengers God was sending to me.

Messengers, those sweet gifts we are offered, come in all sorts of ways. This time messages were sent – and thankfully received – through human kinship as well as little ice crystals forming on naked tree branches. Even an ice storm brought me messages that I needed and offered lessons for me to acknowledge.

Are you paying attention to the messengers in your life? Do not miss out on these gifts which offer inspiration, love, and encouragement. It is fairly easy to figure out if they are a God-given message or not; everything about the message is designed to help you. Trust your instincts; move on if you should. God will place the right people, places and things at just the right time – you have to only pay attention.

Three

An offering ... Friends

As I sat and talked to Jim, I admitted to myself that I could no longer live presenting my outside self as happy and slowing fading away on the inside. The way that I saw it, I had two choices: I either buy into the darkness or I search to embrace that happiness I presented to most everyone else, and no longer just survive. It was very obvious to me the whole pretending to survive facade was not working, I knew God had created me to thrive, not just survive in life.

Sometimes we recognize we have lost ourselves and sometimes, as with Jim, it is recognized by someone else. I did know that I could no longer live by faking my happiness, tending to so many other people and their needs and acting like I was this super happy woman who didn't have a care in the world. The days of talking to my family and friends with my smiling ouside self and crying inside were over. I wanted to love myself! I wanted the laughter and smiling to always be genuine.

Great decision, but now what do I do? Sonja worked with a life and business coach, Stacey, and would beg me to give her a call and talk to her about how I was feeling. I would tell Sonja I was too busy, she could not understand me, I should be able to handle this, God will help me through it, and on and on I would go. Sonja kept at me to make the call. I would make as many excuses as I could but the real reason I wouldn't make that call was driven by fear: what does it look like if she can help and even worse, what if she cannot? Then what? What if she can see the "real" me and think I was not worth her time or effort? What if all she did was judge me? What if... I lived in "what ifs" for quite a few weeks all the while thinking that if today was the day that I was going to die, that would be okay because this was getting too hard for me to handle.

I read a story once about a man who was stuck on top of a building during a flood and was praying for God to save him from the rising waters. So God sends a man in a canoe. The man in the canoe yells up to the man on the rooftop, "Jump in!"

"It's okay," the man replies. "God is going to save me," and waves the canoeist off to be on his way.

Next comes a man in a boat and offers to bring him to safety. Once again, from the rooftop, he says, "God is going to save me, I am continuing to pray."

A helicopter comes to pluck him from the roof top and he yells the same thing to that pilot as well. Eventually he drowns and goes to Heaven. He questions God about why he didn't save him. God replied that he had sent a canoe, a boat, and a helicopter; what more did he want!

This is the exact thought that came to mind when Sonja kept badgering me about calling Stacey. I was praying for help and it was all right in front of me. God had been sending people into my life to help me as I was drowning and I was dismissing each one of them waiting on God to come and pluck me from my darkness!

Finally, the moment came when I felt complete hopelessness. I admitted that Jim was right: I did not really love **me**. Heck, I was not even sure who I was; how could I love someone that I did not even know? It was like running into a brick wall and being knocked down with a force so strong that the wind was pushed out of my lungs. As I kept telling myself that my husband, kids, friends and family did not really want to talk to me - it was more out of obligation - I realized I had taken that on as complete truth. I hardly could talk to Steve for fear I would say something that I would regret. I didn't want him to pick up on my sadness. At least I didn't think he could see it; but then again, how could he not? This is just a few of the ways I would berate myself over and over again until my unconscious mind accepted it as the truth.

Out of complete desperation, I made the call to Stacey. If nothing else, I could tell Sonja I was right; I wasn't worth anyone else's effort. I had taken enough of Jim and Sonja's time from them; I am a lost cause! I would describe me as distraught, confused, hopeless and yet defiant; there was still some fight in me or else how could I have made the call?

Turns out, it was an amazing call! As Stacey says, "Welcome to the first day of the rest of your life." I found a glimmer of hope in our conversation. She assured me what I was thinking and feeling was perfectly legitimate. She continued to explain that when we reach a point in our journey where we feel stuck and unable to move forward, we get to make a choice: stay in the miserable place we are calling our life or make the choice to invest in ourselves and accept the help that has been pounding on our door. I realized I had been stuck for so long I was frozen; unable to do anything to help myself.

I hung up from the phone call with Stacey feeling more energy than I had felt in a very long time. The hope I was searching for had landed on my lap with the push of the "send" button.

As I am writing about this time in my life, a song, "Hold Fast" by Mercy Me is playing in the back ground. It says to "hold fast, help is on the way!" No coincidence here!

Although I didn't know what life was going to look like on the next day (do we ever really?), I was in "I've got this" mode, a renewed energy I had not felt in a long, long time. I was going to be the woman God had been calling for so long! I acknowledged I could no longer continue on my secret path of destruction. I had sought help through my parish priest, spiritual director, trusted friends; they were such an essential part of helping me recognize my need to listen to myself and begin changing the thoughts and excuses which were holding me back.

I was now ready to look at the darkness that was "hanging out" and face it head on. I knew I had finally opened my eyes, ears, heart and soul, all in unison, and hope was born!

Therefore, from the day we heard this, we do not cease praying for you and asking that you may be filled with the knowledge of his will through all spiritual wisdom and understanding o live in a manner worthy of the Lord, so as to be fully pleasing, in every good work bearing fruit and growing in the knowledge of God. Colossians 1:9-10

God truly places people in our life at exactly the right time to learn lessons that will enrich our life. As I write my story, I am recalling a parent who yelled and screamed at me as we tried to work toward a solution. I could give all the details but at the end of the day, I am called to learn from the experience. It took me about a week to figure it out, but I know that experience made me look at my baggage that I brought into the conversation. This woman will probably never know that I completely understood her position, but I was responsible for upholding the integrity of the program for which I was in charge. The most valuable lesson I have learned is that when I feel conflict rising inside myself, I need stop the conversation, have an honest talk with myself, and become very curious what it is that has struck such a nerve. It is so important that I be aware of and own those emotions prior to dealing with conflict. It is only then that I will be able to negotiate a reasonable solution.

Since the situation was not resolved in an agreeable manner, I needed to look at the conflict and learn from the experience. I had training in negotiating and conflict resolution so the tools were there to engage in meaningful conversation. I was not able to use them because I had not factored into the situation my personal baggage. I consider this an extremely valuable lesson as I travel my *Journey of Intention*!

Previously, I would have completely avoided talking to this person. As it was, I had put the conversation off for a couple of weeks. What I failed to do was take a look as to why I was putting it off. Had I spent time thinking about why I was neglecting to dial the number, I would have realized my unconscious mind was telling me one thing while my conscious mind just wanted to avoid conflict. Because I have made incredible strides in understanding and accepting myself, I did not have those conversations of self-doubt and beat myself up over what I should or should not have said or done. I trust that I have gained valuable wisdom that will help me to help someone who crosses my path in the future. This is a whole new level of love for myself which I am confident has never existed prior in my life.

Once again, there are no coincidences, only opportunities put in our paths to offer growth, love and acceptance of ourselves. Our God is an amazing God!

My team as I call them, each played a very important role in helping and assisting me to overcome, basically, myself.

47

I lived each day blaming other people, circumstances, or events in my life as the reason why I felt like I did. and in the next breath, complaining I did not understand why I felt like I did.

Then came a day of breakthrough, it is pivotal in my journey and pushed me in the direction of moving forward of living with intention. I was (again) complaining to Stacey about my inability to understand my thoughts and feelings. It was always important to me to know the why of my life. Why did I feel this way? Why can't I talk to Steve? Why don't my kids act like they want to have a relationship with me? Why do I not feel like my work was ministry anymore? Why? Why? On and on I went: Stacey listened as I rambled. All of a sudden I blurted out to Stacey: "Oh my God, I am the **common denominator** in all of this!"

Silence followed. After I got past the initial shock of the truth of what I said, I had to laugh. On many occasions at work I look at a situation or an issue and consider the common denominator, the consistent factor that is at the center of the issue. Once discovered, I can work towards a solution. I had totally missed this in my personal life. Yes, I was at the middle, the *common denominator* if you will, of all my distress.

I was at the center of all my sadness, confusion, and lack of self love. It was me! It was not important to understand the why of it all; the importance lies in accepting the moments as opportunities to learn, to become curious about those feelings. I was finally ready to hear the words of my coach. All those conversations with Sonja and Jim had a new realization. Although conversations had taken place many times prior to this one with Stacey, I was not able to hear because I was not ready to grow and move forward. I had not learned the lessons needed to accept them with love and a desire to grow. I had, instead, used them to beat myself up psychologically, which resulted in a lack of respect for myself.

As I blurted out to Stacey, I had an "aha" moment that I felt throughout my entire body. I was a little shocked at what I just revealed but most of all curious! As I reflect on that moment, I find it hard to express how I felt. It was as if I was hit by a car and experiencing total freedom all in the same moment. I felt this huge weight lifted from my shoulders yet fully understanding there was work to be done and acknowledging I was up for the journey!

I learned that day that I had lived being the person others expected me to be; at least the person I thought everyone wanted me to be. The attentive wife, the available mom, the dutiful daughter, the friend who was always there when needed, and the employee who worked way too long so as not to go home; those were my survival methods. I decided in that moment it was no longer going to be how I defined myself. I really didn't know what I was going to look like, but I did know it was going to be closer to an authentic version of me. I was no longer going to survive, I was going to thrive!

In a very quick moment I was disappointed because I had failed to see what now seemed so obvious. Then I thought, "Big deal!" I was so thankful I no longer felt like I was sinking in quick sand. I no longer looked back with regret; I chose to reflect upon my past knowing I did the best I could with the tools I had at the time. Looking back on forty plus years of my life, I would not trade a day because I now understand that I was exactly where I needed to be to grow into the woman I am today.

People always show up when we most need them. We
have to do our part: take advantage of the gifts as they are
presented to us on our journey. Are you hanging out on a
rooftop somewhere and missing the people God is sending to
help, guide, and love you through your darkness? Is it time in
your life to seek a deeper understanding of who you are or are
not? Do you really want to make the most of who you are
called to be in this amazing life with which you have been
gifted? Don't stay on the rooftop waiting for God to answer
your prayers when the entire time He is doing just that!

Four

An Offering ... Survival

Where you go, you follow. The first time I heard that statement I really didn't get it. There were so many times I just wanted to leave my life, run away. In my desperation to run, run, run, I would sit and think about what I thought my life would be like if I lived by myself in solitude. I could envision myself in a little tiny apartment with nothing more than a bed, dresser, and some food to eat. (Let's be real, notice I didn't say any cooking utensils; even in my vision I didn't like to cook!)

I had few clothes and no TV. I would sit by the window looking out into the world. As I watched life going by for all the people out walking, heading out to work, and kids playing, I would think to myself, "Is there life out there for me?" I didn't want to join in the hustle and bustle of life; I certainly wasn't into the joy and laughter that I imagined still existed. That only existed for others, not me.

As I allowed my imagination to roam, I would have an occasional close friend or two stop by and check on me. I would invite them into my simple, sparse apartment; we would chat, and they would leave satisfied that I was okay. After all, even in my imagination, I was good at hiding what I truly felt. Occasionally, someone would stop by seeking some kind of advice, we would talk for a while, and they would leave feeling better about some deep insight that would be life changing for them.

These reoccurring thoughts would show up many times over several months. Whenever I thought running away would be the answer, I saw myself as a lonely woman, feeling helpless about her poor pathetic life.

In the very next instant, I would feel guilty. Once again I called myself selfish; how could I even think that I had problems. There were women in the world who were being mistreated by their spouses, kids not knowing where their next meal was coming from, and dads who could not find a job to support their family. And then I would be good for a while ... until I wasn't.

I do not remember the exact moment; however, somewhere along the way, I realized the truth to the statement: you can run, but you cannot hide. I had been planning a retreat in the Smokey Mountains for almost six months. My spiritual director kept encouraging me to go. I would listen to her amazing revelations she encountered every time she would have the experience and think about how I want those kinds of revelations in my life, too.

So, off I went. My son and his wife lived in North Carolina at the time, so I decided to go a couple of days early and spend time with them. I was looking forward to the fourteen-hour drive, listening to my music and running away from it all; yes, **running**. I have to be honest; I did enjoy the solitude of the drive. I remember laughing to myself that I had my own personal concert from *Third Day*, my favorite Christian band. They serenaded me through four or five states. I sang, danced in my seat and enjoyed every moment of the drive. I thought, "Yeah, this is what I need." I enjoyed the weekend tremendously, spending way overdue time with the kids. It was just us, doing whatever we liked, and seeing the beauty of North Carolina. Soon enough, I was headed down the road to the retreat center.

As I got closer to the small town of Maggie Valley, North Carolina, I felt an anxiousness that was unfamiliar. What was I to expect? What if the big "boom" I was looking for didn't happen? What if I got lost in the mountains? What if everyone there thinks I'm crazy? What? What? What? "Oh good Lord," I said to myself, "Relax."

I pulled into the very practical building nestled at the bottom of the mountains and I felt a wave of calm come over me. I met Sr. Ann who had a gentle, kind smile. She said she had been waiting for me. ("Why, did someone call and tell you to make sure I arrived in one emotional piece?") I began to relax as I settled into my sweet little room. There was nothing grand about the place and that was just perfect.

Throughout the week our routine was to eat breakfast, gather for prayer, and listen to a reflection by Sr. Ann who would then give a focus for the day. We would then go to the mountains and wander around all day. About three o'clock we would come back together, travel back down the mountain, celebrate Mass, eat and have a final gathering and reflection before heading back to our rooms. Doesn't that sound like heaven?

The first day I went up to the mountains and began hiking, never stopping until I ate lunch. I had my music in my ears and just moved. I was afraid to sit still and be silent. I remember thinking, "God, I am in no mood to listen to anything you have to say to me today." I was really afraid of what might come to my heart; fearful that I would not be able to handle the flood of emotions, thoughts, and fears.

We carpooled each day; the man I was with was one of the kindest men I have ever met. He was a Brother in an order of priests. The order of brothers live simply to serve others. He thought about becoming a priest but felt this better suited what God called him to. The difference between his calling and that of a priest is he does not celebrate Mass and cannot hear confessions.

Most days it was just the two of us. We talked about life, his and mine. He had been through quite an ordeal with his health when he was a young man. He came to understand how blessed he was to be alive, now nearing retirement. We talked about the breakdown in the family today. He felt like everything in our society and its problems stem from the lack of commitment and forgiveness between husband and wife. He had worked with many families and spoke strictly from his experience. He would ask me what I thought about the state of our world. The first time he asked, I was like, "The state of the world? I cannot even figure out my state!" Wow! This was hitting home! How could he know? Did he know I was running away from my family for the week? That I was running away from work, friends, everything?

As the week went on I began to think of him as an angel, sent to me personally by God Himself! How blessed was I that I would deserve this kind of intervention: a man of God who was kind, compassionate, non-judgmental, and accepting. By the end of day two I was looking more forward to the rides up the mountain to see what the angel had to say than the trek in the mountains itself.

By day three I had taken my ear phones out of my ears and began to listen to the voices of the forest: rushing water flowing through clear streams that have been flowing for hundreds of years; birds chirping their sweet tunes; trees taller that any I have seen back home swaying back and forth like they were keeping beat to music that only the animals of the forest could hear. The flowers, wild we call them, provided such splendor for each hiker to walk by and appreciate the simplicity of its exquisiteness.

As I hiked through the mountains on one of the chilly, glorious days, I came across an old cemetery. I sat down and had lunch with the eternal neighbors buried together in a small space in the vast mountains. Most graves were not marked; for at least a couple of hundred years they had been lying side by side in the peaceful mountains surrounded by brush, trees, wooden markers and evidence of old fence posts that marked the sacred space. I reflected about what life had been like for them. I did not know if they were the native tribe of the area or perhaps settlers who didn't make it through the winter cold. I wondered if it was a family grave. What would I want someone to think of my life if they came across my old tombstone in a couple of hundred years?

I pondered the thought for a number of hours. I thought about all the amazing people I have in my life and those I have yet to meet. I decided I would want the sojourners to think I was a joy-filled person; ambitious in life and mission; I loved and was loved. I would want them to know I had grown into a woman who had learned to love herself, mistakes, blessings and all. Most of all, I would want them to know that during my time on earth I made the world a better place for all who crossed my path. Could we ever ask for more than to know we have made others lives better because we mentored, loved, and accepted them for the person they wish to be?

Somewhere in those thoughts, I began to realize that I had become so disconnected with nature; I no longer recognized the beauty of simply being present in the moment being provided for me. I thought about how the gift of nature is a gift from God. Through my disconnect, I had also became disengaged from my God. I had lost trust in the One who is the unconditional lover I was always seeking.

This wasn't the big "boom" I had expected. I was hoping to be struck down with great thunder and hear God speak His words of wisdom to me! Isn't that what an "aha" moment was like? As usual, God knows better. Coming to understand that God is always present, at all times in all situations, was in of itself a reminder of "Trust me."

I wonder if I had not had this experience, would I have taken notice of those life-changing ice crystals months later?

God is our refuge and our strength, an ever-present help in distress. Thus we do not fear, though earth be shaken and mountains quake to the depths of the sea, though its waters rage and foam and mountains totter at its surging. Psalm 46:1-3

As a teacher, I had taught that same message of trusting and relying on God and His love for each of us to my students for many years; but now it was no longer just words; it was my own understanding of God that I could grasp, feel, love, and understand! I did not need to run from life! I needed to run *to* my life!

It took me several months to process all that I learned and experienced in the Smokies. I still go back there sometimes in my mind. However, now it is not to experience running away. I reflect and feel empowered to continue on my own little sojourn. There was still a lot of work ahead, but I knew I would survive if I kept being honest with myself and moving forward.

During the beginning of my intentional journey, I visited for several months with my pastor, Fr. Dan. We talked about my childhood, getting married so young, my 25-year four-year degree (yes, it took me 25 years to finish college!), my son in the Army, my family living away and mostly my response to all of this. He explained to me that my reaction to all of these life moments was a survival technique. That's how people survive situations in their lives like abuse, abandonment, fear, living with alcoholic parents, divorce, and the list goes on; you can fill in your blank. For some, it might be drinking to mask the pain, for others it may be ignoring or pretending to live a different life. His point was we do some things as a means of survival. For me, it was always pretending to be this happy, go-lucky woman and keeping the feelings of immense sadness and constant self-doubt to myself.

I had some experiences in my life for which I just was never ready to forgive myself, to seek to understand, or to accept the situation for what it was. It never occurred to me that we are all broken to some degree; sometimes we choose to put humpty-dumpty together, and sometimes we choose misery to be our place of comfort. Whatever the decision, we talked about it as a survival technique until either we are ready to deal with it, or it no longer works for us. It was both for me. I was tired of faking it; I wanted that joy that I knew existed inside of me. I knew it because I had experienced it in varying doses many times throughout my life.

Fr. Dan explained that because I was not yet ready to emotionally deal with all my "stuff," I lived making excuses about it all. He backed up what Stacey and Jim had been saying. His words and timing were obviously different. I was hiding the real me so no one would be more the wiser. (Isn't that what we always think; that no one can tell?)

While we were talking one afternoon, I vividly recall Fr. Dan holding up one fist and wrapping his hand around the other. He explained this is us fitting in the mold that other people expect of us. He then opened his fist up and spread his fingers out just a bit and explained this is us trying to break away from the mold. We try it for a while, get scared, and go back into the mold (moving his hand back around the fist). It's what we know and where we somehow find comfort; at least we know we will survive. We know we will survive because we are alive at that moment. As I leaned back in the chair and intently listened to him, I was struck by the reality of how true that was! I had been allowing myself to be molded by what I perceived were others expectations of how I should act, think, and even feel. How many times have I heard the statement, "We can only hear when we are ready to receive the message?" I heard loud and clear in that conversation.

It is like I would dip a toe, may be two toes, into a pool of water. I would always decide the water was too cold and pull away. Occasionally, I might jump in but then quickly decide I might drown; so out I would climb, going back into the warmth of that fist. I feared a lot of things in my life: I wasn't smart enough worth the effort, and I especially was not loveable.

Taking 25 years to complete my bachelor education is an example of my lack of self-confidence. I would attend college for a semester or two taking a couple of classes. Then I would stop for a semester or two. I could excuse it (and I did) saying Steve was out of town too much, the kids were too involved in extra activities, or I worked too much. Occasionally, I would have an instructor that was so critical of my work that I would use that as an excuse not to return. (See, I was dumb!) I understand now those were just excuses, but at that time it was where I was. This was one of those places where I held myself to a higher standard. As soon as I wiggled, I would stop going to school. Eventually, I would jump back in and repeat the cycle.

As I sat and listened to Fr. Dan, I decided in that very instant I was shattering the mold of my old self. Shattering. Not just walking away. I reasoned if it is shattered it cannot be put back together. I would have to start anew. Some days I would catch myself sliding back towards that mold and then I would remember: it no longer exists. I had shattered the mold many months before and I understood there was no going back. I was not rooted in fear; I was rooted in empowerment! I realized this was another step that I chose to become intentional in my journey and began revealing more of ME to myself.

Have you lived your life in fear? Do you keep running back into the safety of the mold that you have created for yourself? Or was your mold created for you? You go back to the "safe place" because you know that you can survive life if you stay there. My challenge to you is, do you want to survive at life or thrive? I am all about thriving and running to life as opposed to surviving and running away from life!

Five

An Offering ... Wisdom

As a young child, I would often ask God to grant me the gift of wisdom. I did not name it as such; more like, "Help me to be a nice person, be kind to my friends, help me to understand about others," that sort of asking. I have come to understand that God has answered my prayer many times over. I smile as I write this because you know the saying, "Be careful what you ask for." It is just now that I am embracing, accepting and using the gift of wisdom that has been granted to me throughout the years, most all of my life.

I have acquired wisdom through learning from others: their mistakes, tragedies, and joyful moments. When I was just a young fifth grade student, I lost a classmate to a heart defect. Imagine as a ten-year-old child receiving a phone call that Johnny did not make it through the surgery we had been told would be a simple procedure. We had celebrated life with him, gifting him with a baseball bat and glove so he would be able to play ball with us in the fall. Our class made plans to start the next school year using him as the pitcher; he had waited so long to be a participant in our lunch time games as opposed to cheerleader for our team. This is one of those moments that stands frozen in my mind; receiving the news of his death and not really knowing what to do or how to understand it all.

School was out for the summer; we could not mourn together as a class and share memories like we so often do when a loved one dies. I did not realize at that tender age I was acquiring wisdom: an intimate understanding of death, one I hoped my own children would never have to experience. Although that was not to be; they experienced the death of their grandfather early in their young life. Through the experience of my earlier years, I understood the importance of sitting down with them and talking through the emotions and questions of young hearts. "Where is Papaw now?" "Will I ever see him again?" "How come he had to die?"

Mourning together as community or family is essential to healing; I also knew the significance of not hiding them from the sadness and pain of others. I made sure they were around family and friends while we gathered at the funeral home and celebrated his life at church. We have always spoken of him sharing our memories. He loved our children and I never want them to lose that feeling of being loved by their grandfather. Wisdom I acquired so many years earlier showed itself in the greatest time of need for our family.

Wisdom also comes the hard way: making choices that I regret, ignoring my intuition, and thinking I know better than my mentors and teachers. As I reflect on the regrets, I realize mistakes remain mistakes only if I do not choose to grow from the experience. I can sit around and play the blame game or I can face the reality of choices or circumstances and move on to a better place. Sometimes those choices or circumstances were not because of my involvement; I was just on the receiving end. There is always something learned that brings me to be a better, stronger or perhaps more compassionate person. I can say this now because I have acquired the wisdom that it takes for me to learn and move forward.

I once worked with a man, who for reasons I do not know, just did not like me. It would really upset me that he would try to make me look like a fool or make sure to point out my mistakes in front of others. This was the first time I had ever encountered someone who would rather see me fail and enjoy watching me fail than to support the mission of my ministry. I did not understand it; I was at a loss as how to handle him, or myself for that matter.

A very wise woman (my secretary) challenged me to turn the pain and hurt I felt from his viciousness into pity for him. I remember vividly sitting at my desk whining about his behavior. She turned around and said, "I have some thought (wisdom?) I would like to share." I swung my chair around and looked at her and seeing the compassion and kindness in her eyes, I knew she was sincere in her words. Unconsciously I was getting something out of this anger; if nothing else, I thought I was gaining some kind of upper hand being angry at him. It was like I believed he was suffering because of my anger. I was so lost in my own misery that I could not see what she could: he could care less about how I was reacting; he had his own agenda and his own issues.

Honestly, I really thought about ignoring the advice my secretary offered. Instead, I looked up "pity" in the dictionary. I remember part of the definition saying "show mercy." At first I was like, "Not happening." Then I thought about how my secretary was such a wise woman who always reacted with love. I had such respect and love for her. I knew in that moment she was mentoring me in a life-long lesson: it is far better to have mercy for those who wish you harm. You lose nothing and gain freedom.

I began focusing less on him and more on my goals. I was free from his useless words and actions. Once I really gave my anger and hurt over to pity, I was in a much better place emotionally and spiritually. I was more effective in my ministry and erred on the side of empathy when crossing paths with him. I did what I knew was best for me; he had to deal with himself and his own personal agenda. I understand now that people all have their own challenges and doors they walk through. By dealing with the "me" part of this situation, I removed myself from his drama. It was so much healthier for me.

I understand that which I did not years before: in all likelihood the reaction he had towards me was a result of some deep seated experience in his past. I just triggered it for whatever reason; the result being a difficult working relationship. I do not lay all blame on him, however, I carried my own insecurities about my ability to lead, coming into new community, trying to fit in, all the while still having an occasional pity party about having to leave my former community because Steve got transferred in his work. It was really quite a blessing to learn so much and gain such wisdom from a wise woman and a bitter man. Both taught me valuable lessons; I could say one lesson was easier than the other, but I am not sure that is true. She taught me the value and the understanding of 'pity.' He gave me the experience of using pity as means of forgiving and moving forward.

I can only hope I am given mercy, or pity, when the shoe is on the other foot. Previously, I would run from conflict as opposed to work toward a solution. I only knew to run from myself instead of to myself. If I understood ten years ago what I understand now, the first question I would have asked myself was, "What about this is about me?" The answer to the question would have been something like, "You are not feeling comfortable in your position because you are new to the community and not fully confident in your leadership abilities." From there, I would seek out the help or training I needed. I would not have been concerned about his anger that was directed at me.

Get wisdom, get understanding! Do not forget or turn aside from the words of my mouth. Do not forsake her, and she will preserve you; love her, and she will safeguard you; The beginning of wisdom is: get wisdom; whatever else you get, get understanding. Proverbs 4:6-7

It doesn't matter how old I am, I am constantly learning; or should I say, gaining wisdom. As a grown woman, I became friends with a person who eventually became a source of an unhealthy, or what I call, a toxic relationship. I had moved into a new community and neighborhood. I was very lonely. I would take my kids to school, come home, sit on the couch looking at pictures of past friends and family I left back in the Midwest, and cry. When it came time to get the kids from school, I would dry up and head out. Oh, it was a wonderful pity party. One day in the mist of my "partying" I looked around my house and thought, "No one else is coming to the party – I better get over it."

I connected with a lady from the neighboring town. I was given gifts, taken to lunch, and shared a lot of time together while the kids were at school. I was also privy to the gossip that was generously shared. This was gossip on steroids! I know I used that gossip to judge other people. I knew that this was not a positive situation for me to be a part of but I just wasn't prepared for the loneliness I thought would be right around the corner if I lost this one and only friend. I eventually took a job at a school but kept in constant contact with my friend.

While at a convention, a co-worker I was traveling with said to me, "I am going to say something to you and I don't want us to talk about it until tomorrow. Just think about it." She then looked at me and said, "Toxic friendship." She said good night and walked to her room. I went into my room and thought about the word "toxic." I knew whom she was talking about.

As I sat in the hotel room, I thought about what poison does to a body. If we ingest toxins or poisons in small doses, we might experience numbness somewhere in our body, or be a little forgetful; maybe we even ignore the symptoms at first. Then, as the poison continues to travel through our body, we become lethargic, maybe even lifeless. Eventually if enough poison is in our body, we die. Wow!

Processing that reality in the context of the unhealthy friendship that I was taking part was another one of the "aha" moments. It was time to move on past my fears of loneliness and make some healthy decisions for myself.

Funny thing about only having this one friend was once I walked away (literally) from the relationship, I gained so many more friends. I actually had someone come up to me and tell me they would have loved to have befriended me earlier but I was *her* friend. Ouch!

My regret is that I just walked away, avoided and ignored the friendship. At that point in my life, I did not have the tools nor the confidence to say what needed to be said. Truthfully, like I have previously said, I allowed fear to prevail. Perhaps my words of honesty could have made a difference in her life as well as mine. Maybe not, but I will never know because I didn't take the opportunity to use them. Later, when I would look back at those years, I would beat myself up, telling myself, after all, I was an adult; how could I have allowed myself to participate in a friendship which was unhealthy? For heaven's sake, it wasn't like I was in junior high school; I was an adult woman!

It is in this experience I recognized that sometimes friendships are seasonal. They come in our life to teach us something very valuable; and then we must move on to the next part of our journey, using what we learned in order to make our world a better place for ourselves, which in turn makes a better world for others. That very brief friendship and conversation I had with my co-worker at the convention proved to be hugely important in my life. She came to me (or was she sent?) and delivered her message which resulted in an amazing life lesson for me. Yes, sometimes friendships are seasonal; but significant nonetheless.

One of the ways the "toxic friendship" experience has blessed me is in my time spent as a classroom teacher. I recognize the symptoms of unhealthy friendships as they begin forming in the classroom. It does not surprise me that kids get involved in toxic friendships. I know intimately the feeling of not belonging, being on the outside, and not having confidence in myself. In junior high school those disbeliefs are rampant. If they do not think about the negative images themselves, their peers are sure to point it out to them. We tend to look for acceptance anywhere when we are not in friendship with our self. Most kids do not realize they are in a situation which is not healthy for them; they just want the feeling of belonging. Through this gift of wisdom, I do not ignore students when I suspect this behavior is occurring. I use all the tools at my disposal to teach the importance and value of each person. Personal stories are the best teachers and I have plenty! Using metaphors, the students relate to is an effective means to help them recognize themselves somewhere in the story. Ultimately, like all of us, the student must be willing to learn. If the heart is not open to what we are called to learn, the fall is hard and often repeated.

I have also acquired wisdom the right way – trusting my intuition, having faith in God and making decisions that were rooted in thought and prayer. My son is in the United States Army. I have always supported his career choice realizing he is living his passion and accepting this as his purpose in life. I assure you, however, it is not without fear. It is two strange emotions to have at the same time: fear and being proud of your child, all in the same breath.

The first time my son went to Afghanistan I was a complete mess. I could not even say the words, 'son' and 'Afghanistan' in the same sentence without breaking down. I was frozen in fear and stuck in an emotional roller coaster. I used to say I was being forced to join a club that I did not want to join. That club being moms who were so proud of the kids but lived this reality of when someone dressed in a uniform might show up at your doorstep. As I became one of "those moms," I was like a little kid who was being led to school for the first day kicking and screaming, "No, no I won't go!" But, just like the kids who were tugged and sometime dragged to school, go I did. I could not have been more proud; I could not have been more fearful.

One night as I was driving home from work in the dark, I was feeling the effects of the long, cold winter. Steve was out of town so I knew I was going home to a dark house. I kept hearing the little voice inside my head telling me not to go home; I was not in a good place emotionally thinking about my son and war; I was really going to lose it. In the same thought, really, where was I going to go? To my friend's house and say hey, this little voice is telling me not to go home? So, I went home to the dark house, walked in with my arms full of stuff from work, dropped it all on the floor and started crying. Pleading. Begging. Bargaining. All those things we do in our most desperate moments with God. I banged my hands on the counter and reminded God what an amazing kid he is and how he is going to change the world. Remember God?

My poor little dog just sat and looked up at me with her sad eyes staring into my tear-stained face. She could not figure out if she should be happy to see me or just not move for fear I would become more hysterical. I think she was shocked for a moment. I can still see the fear and protection of me in her sweet little eyes.

I decided the best thing to do was to run a tub of bubbles and hot water. As the tub filled with bubbles, I began to turn all the pleading, begging and bargaining into prayer. I started thanking God for all that is good and honorable in our world. I began asking for strength and courage, the true gifts of God's love for me. In all of one second, I felt this huge weighted burden that had been sitting on my shoulders lift up and disperse into the air! I get the chills just thinking about it now. I know in that moment God took from me and absorbed into Himself, all my fear and pain I had been hanging on to for many, many months. It was as if He was saying, "I got this, just trust me." As so I do, trust in God and lay all those burdens at His feet. I know His Devine plan is greater than any of my human fear. It is one of my greatest truths, even though time and time again I must remind myself. I share this story so that you will hand to God what is God's: your pain, worry, fear. Let Him carry those burdens with you. I guarantee it is a lot lighter!

I now recognize these were holy moments given to me by my God for moments of gained wisdom. These are just the moments I gained paying attention; I cannot imagine all the ones I have missed! All those years ago as a little girl as I prayed for wisdom, God answered time and time again. I didn't grasp it at first. However, I am ever thankful, and amazed.

How have you gained wisdom in your life? Was the growth through the stories and experiences of others? Maybe your experiences have been gained like some of mine, you know, the hard way? However the wisdom is gained, it is that we accept wisdom as wisdom, not a failure or a mistake. Accept it as an opportunity to become intentional in your journey.

Six

An offering ... Forgiveness

Because the judgments you give are the judgments you will get, and the standard you use will be the standard used for you. Why do you observe the splinter in your brother's eye and never notice the great log in your own? And how dare you say to your brother, "Let me take that splinter out of your eye," when, look, there is a great log in your own? Hypocrite! Take the log out of your own eye first, and then you will see clearly enough to take the splinter out of your brother's eye. Matthew 7:2-5

Since beginning my *Journey of Intention*, I have focused a lot of energy on forgiveness. What is it exactly? Is it I feel so bad because I have hurt someone and am tired of carrying around all the guilt? Or is it I want the person who hurt me to hurt as much as me, so I will not forgive him? Fair is fair, right? If it is *fair,* then why do I not thrive in life? Something must need fixing.....that something is forgiveness: giving, receiving, and accepting.

This chapter has been the most difficult chapter to write. There are so many different aspects to forgiving: the act of forgiving; receiving forgiveness; accepting forgiveness and truly forgiving the transgressor: the loss of actually living because of grudges; and ultimately accepting, really accepting, that God is a forgiving God, an unconditional, loving, forgiving God. I have struggled with each one of these.

Recently I was watching a video on the inspiration behind a song that Christian song writer and singer Matthew West sings called, "Forgiveness." It brought me to tears. A mom lost one of her twin daughters and her daughter's friend because a young man was driving drunk. He was eventually sentenced to 22 years in jail. Through the process of healing, the mom forgave the young man. Most of the members of her family followed suit and forgave him as well. The story doesn't end there; she went to court on his behalf to ask that his sentence be reduced. Still the story does not end; this family has embraced this young man as a member of their own family! How can that be possible? It is an incredible story of forgiveness and healing. Does this act of forgiveness lessen the love the mother has for her child? Does this fill the void where the deep pain lies? No and No.

Through her unfathomable pain and grief, everyone gave her permission to hate the young man. Even the justice system granted the go-ahead. The mom commented on it in the video, like that was going to somehow be the cure for her bitterness and hurt. She made a choice that allowed her to move forward and to share her message with many other people. As the forgiver, I can only imagine what the process was like for her: she had her pride to consider; after all, what does it say about her if she forgives this young man? Is she weak? Has she lost the love she felt for her daughter? What will other people think? God wouldn't blame her if she doesn't forgive that boy, would He?

What about the young man? He made the choice to drink and drive; why does he deserve forgiveness? Does he feel guilt? Shame? He deserves what he has coming! If these are your thoughts, I doubt that he would have disagreed with you. He made a terrible decision that resulted in a horrible outcome: the deaths of two beautiful young women and the destruction of not one, not even two, but three families at the very least.

The mother did not forgive the young man for his sake; it was for her own healing. She realized at some point this was about her. She needed to move back to life and hope. The only way that was going to happen for her was to forgive the unforgivable.

> *"I apply Christ to your account. His death satisfies what your offense deserves in a way nothing else can... even my anger or revenge. I see in our relationship a picture of my attempt to be reconciled to God. My actions created a hopeless situation until Christ took my place so in our relationship I will allow Him to take your place."* **Brad Hambrick**

I have found this statement to be very powerful; I have read and reread it over and over again. It is profound. Praying these very words, inserting the name of my offender and releasing these emotions that are tied in my inability to move forward gives me the chance to live again. What an opportunity! Do I dare insert my name as if the one I offended was praying this for me?

One of the most challenging times for me is when I would not forgive myself. I have been told (okay, I know this for fact!) that I would hold myself to such impossible standards; I expect absolute perfection in my work, home and even play life. When I would not meet those standards, I would begin swirling around words in my head that absolutely paralyzed me: you are dumb, lazy, don't try hard enough, a jerk, ineffective as a leader, mean boss, too fat, and on and on. I was aware this was going on inside of my mind, but I just thought it was "normal" and the right way to correct my imperfections. I have always been harder on myself; I would never express these thoughts to someone else in their struggles. Like I said, impossible standards.

As a Christian, I would always embrace that God forgives our sins. Intellectually, we all get that, right? I believed I saw that as the easy part. My faith teaches me Jesus did the impossible to believe: accepted death as a means for me to have life. (Does he know how often I mess up?) I accept the gift of forgiveness when given to me by another person, myself, or by God. Or, do I?

I met Sonja on the first day of high school. I was not happy about starting another new school in yet another new community. I decided in my ninth grade maturity that I would just go through the motions for the next four years – if I was lucky enough to actually go to the same school for my entire high school experience. I had attended five schools during my primary education. I was really mad that my dad moved us to Missouri; I had a great experience in junior high and wanted to continue that "fun." I was a band member and had a great future (in my 8th grade reality) as a leading member of the high school marching band. That was my mind set as I walked onto the campus on the first day of high school.

As I stood in a line, Sonja walked up and introduced herself; it turned out she lived in my neighborhood. We became friends immediately, played volleyball, and ran around like all kids in high school. We would hang out, then go different directions and eventually reconnect again, pretty much like all young people do as they search for their identity and friendship groups. She thrived in high school. She had moved a year before me but she was happy to have moved. I had to leave all my friends behind knowing I would never see them again. She helped me realize this high school experience in Missouri might not be so bad after all.

Seems like a long time ago, yet only yesterday.

We graduated soon enough. I got married shortly after graduation; Sonja began working in various capacities and going to school. We didn't run around a lot but kept in touch and hung out when we could. One bright, beautiful day, she came by and asked if I wanted to go with her to buy some new clothes for her new job. Since I was never one to pass up a shopping trip, off we went. On our way home, Sonja shared a very personal part of her life, something she had been discerning for quite some time, and I was one of the privileged few she was sharing it with.

In her vulnerability, I totally couldn't accept what she was telling me. I shut down emotionally. I didn't show it at that very moment, but once I was at home, I got caught up in my judging her and thinking there was really something wrong with her. I made her situation about **me** and how **I** felt. I didn't reach out to her, ignored phone calls, would not answer the door when she came by; I eventually broke ties with her. This is very difficult for me to share, certainly not my finest friend moment.

I was repeating what had always been my history: run, run, run; judge and avoid. Eventually, Sonja moved on to another city. I kept track of her off and on through other friends. I never contacted her. Life went on. It was easy for me to push the emotions into the back of my mind. This is how I always handled emotions when they were raw. Really, all I had to do was bury the pain, hurt, grief, etc., put a smile on my face, and carry on my life. I did not even know I was in such a state of denial! It was what I knew how to do and, therefore, it is what I did!

On a visit back home, she called to say she was in town and could she come over for a visit. I will never forget opening the door and seeing her standing there; she said she had to have a drink or two in order to get the courage to come over.

That moment, leaning against my door, looking at Sonja, hearing her say she had to drink in order to feel confident to come to my home, was a defining moment in my life. I could not believe that I was "that person" who judged others. This was the girl who had been my friend since the day I stepped onto the campus at high school; my best friend for heaven's sake.

Standing at the door that evening, I also realized how I had made this all about **me**. Throughout the years when I would allow myself to be alone with my deepest thoughts, I struggled with the guilt of knowing she had come to me, confided in me, and I just ran. I remember thinking, "What kind of person am I really?" I was a Christian; is this the way I am supposed to react? I was ashamed of myself.

We talked for quite a while about so much and yet so little. I do not remember if she actually said, "I forgive you" that night, but I knew her showing up was, at the very least, her unspoken words alluding to just that: I forgive you. There were so many thoughts running through my head as we parted ways that night. Mostly, the thought of how I had made this all about me. What about Sonja? She is the one who was really hurt. She is the one who trusted in our friendship. She is the one who was vulnerable.

And then she is the one who forgave. I did not even know I needed forgiveness until that moment. Remember, it was still about me.

After that evening, we would connect whenever she was back in town as well as occasionally talk on the phone. We didn't spend a lot of energy talking about "that time." I did, however, realize that Sonja displayed more vulnerability, courage and honesty than I have ever experienced in a friendship; and she *offered* **me** forgiveness. I thought that I had accepted that blessed gift from her.

Years later, when we were talking about "that time," I asked her why she forgave me. By now, I was well on my *Journey of Intention*; I had begun wrestling with this whole thought of forgiveness; not just with her but in my many experiences of life where I either forgave, needed to forgive, and accepted (or not) forgiveness.

I can see that conversation as vividly as if it were yesterday. "Sonja, why did you forgive me when I had hurt you so much?" I asked.

"Because I knew that was not who you truly were."

"Really?" I asked in surprise.

"Yes, I knew *you* were not reacting, you were answering in a way (perhaps) society said you should respond. I knew better."

She could see in me what I could not: I was worthy pf her forgiveness. Even in that conversation I was not sure who I was, but by then, I was on my path to find out. I was ready to hear her words of forgiveness. What a gift!

When Sonja initially forgave me, I do not think I truly accepted the gift she gave so freely. It was years later when she said, "that is not who you truly were," that I allowed myself to let go of the guilt and shame that I had I claimed as my companions for so long; at least the guilt and shame from this experience.

I was discovering that it was very hard to really come to know myself if I was going to keep carrying around so many negative thoughts and emotions. They were burdens that were getting very heavy; and I was getting tired of carrying them.

My three big influencers were practically working overtime: Sonja supporting me, Jim challenging me to quit being so hard on myself, and Stacey always questioning me so I could gather positive learnings from the past and move on to a future that I desired. I realized I needed some additional spiritual guidance to help me over the next hurdle on my journey. This was taking a huge risk for me. I was going to be, what's the word? Vulnerable. Yeah, that's it. I did not like putting myself in a position of vulnerability. I had to be in control, and the implications of the "v" word meant I could possibly lose control. However, I now was desperate. I could not say it to Steve, but we both knew my relationship with him was suffering. He has always been my support and biggest fan. I was pushing him further and further away with every passing day.

I began talking to Father Dan on a regular basis. The defining moment in our conversations came one day as I walked into his office and just started crying. I could not stop. I don't remember exactly what was flowing through my mind at the moment; I just kept saying I could not forgive myself. Father Dan asked me, "Do you believe God forgives you?"

I looked up and replied, "Yes."

"Really?" he asked as he looked intently into my eyes.

"Of course."

"Wow, you have that kind of power do you?" he said.

"Excuse me?" I asked.

"You just said that you believe God has forgiven you but you cannot forgive yourself. What I hear is that you must have more power than God because you hold onto to something that He has let go long ago." Father Dan just sat there and let the thought sink in for a minute.

I thought about it; if I was hanging on to my pain after knowing God had forgiven me, was this a power play on my part? Did I really think I was more powerful than God? What was I getting out of holding on, not allowing myself forgiveness? There had to be something ...

I looked at him partly in panic ("Me, more powerful than God?"), partly in confusion ("I don't think so!"), and finally, "Welcome back." It was as if God was welcoming me home once again. The prodigal daughter who ran, ran, ran only to return home to find her Father's arms wide open! Most all of my adult life I have been teaching about God's forgiveness and His unconditional love. There is nothing I can do that would cause God to withdraw His love. Yet there I sat, unable to accept the very gift that I had taught so many others about through the years. Wasn't I something?

I have had many conversations with friends about this very topic: our inability to forgive ourselves. I wonder if it is more a matter of us being unwilling to accept the gift of forgiveness which has already been granted. Regardless if the gift is from a human or the Divine, one thing is for sure: we cannot move forward if we dig in our heels and refuse to accept a gift freely given. What a devastating thought; because of my stubbornness, my relationship with God was being affected. How fortunate for me that I discovered the secret of forgiveness before it was too late.

Many years earlier, Sonja forgave me. When I would think about it through the years, I would tell myself that I could not forgive myself. In retrospect, I had not accepted her gift. I had that very same realization when Fr. Dan said those words to me. I knew I did not have more power than God; I had never really accepted His gift.

Sometime later when Sonja and I talked about that part of our history I asked her why she forgave me. She replied, "Because I knew that is not who you really are." She saw in me what I could not see in myself.

As I mentioned earlier, it has been quite a long process for me to write about forgiveness. It is because there were still lessons I needed to learn about myself and even some situations where I would be called to share some of my story and wisdom in order to help others look at their guilt and truly accept forgiveness. I am quite certain there are many more lessons for me to learn; however, now I learn with an awareness that I had not known previously.

A young man came into my office one night at work. He was very troubled and carried the weight of the world on his young shoulders. We sat down and chatted a couple of minutes. As he talked, the words, "I feel so much guilt," spilled out of his mouth. Father Dan popped into my mind. I asked if I could share a personal story. As I told of my conversation with Fr. Dan, it was obvious he could identify with so much of what I was talking about. When I reached the part of my story where I said, "I just cannot forgive myself," he looked at me and shook his head in agreement. I asked him if he felt like God has forgiven him and he said yes. As I explained the whole, "You have more power than God?" part of the story, he had a look of, "Oh my God!" on his face. It was so wonderful to be able to share my experience and know, actually witness, the "aha" moment where truth and understanding fuse together. I saw in the young man what Fr. Dan must have witnessed in me.

I watched that video, "Forgiveness," as I was preparing a talk on forgiveness. That I was asked to talk about forgiveness for a leadership seminar was no accident. I know that is one of the reasons I could not move past this chapter. I had to really look deep into myself and see if I really meant what I was going to share with my audience; I must be authentic. I did a lot of soul searching about how I really felt about forgiveness, both accepting and receiving. I had some really powerful stories I had acquired through wisdom and I knew that if I really meant what I said, I, too, would grow in relationship to God just by sharing my story. It was a great time for a self-check.

It is really "funny" how sometimes I think I have made great strides in a situation or experience, having learned all there was to learn. Then I receive another one of those "gifts." This gift arrived in a package marked "a child's mother" in the form of a phone call at work. Mother was upset and was going to make sure I understood policy needed to change. After a lengthy conversation and no policy change, the phone call ended with both of us upset. How could she not see my side of the issue? She is just bitter! Or was I the one who was bitter? Who does she think she is? Who do I think I am (ouch!)?

Coincidently (not really), it turned out we had a prayer service at work that very same night. As we stood to pray the Lord's Prayer, I thought "oh no! I am going to have to forgive her!" You know the part of the prayer, "Forgive us our trespasses as we forgive those who trespass against us." I knew that I could not say those words out loud, much less pray them in my heart, if I did not mean what I said. So I forgave her in that instant. There have been other times when I thought, "Okay, I will forgive but only because Jesus Christ says I should." This was not one of those times. I knew she was doing the best she could at this point in her life with what she knew, and I was actually glad to forgive her. I realize I cannot control her end of the story; I hope she has reached a place in her journey that calls her to do the same to me, for her sake.

And still no end to the chapter on forgiveness.

Then came the BIG understanding as to the reason I had not been able to move past this chapter. I came to understand that I needed to apologize to Steve for keeping him at arm's length for so many years. I needed to ask for his forgiveness.

As I thought about all the years that I was searching for my individuality and independence, I had pushed and pushed this wonderful man away; it is a wonder he stuck around. Have I mentioned how patient and supportive he is?

Through the years of raising the kids, working, and going to school, I was not about to be vulnerable and have Steve think I was not capable of doing it all. As time passed, I would put my energy in a lot of other places so as not to sit idle for too long or else I would begin to feel guilty about always doing my own thing, not including Steve in many activities or conversations.

As I reflect on all those years, several thoughts come to mind. Number one, that Steve was so patient; when I apologized he just said, "I love you." Wow! Number two, I know I did the very best with where I was at that point in my life. Number three, I know my experience has given me wisdom that I am called to share with you. Hence, this book is written for you. Number four, without these encounters, I would not have been able to have the passion that is ignited inside of my soul and fully understood the purpose for which God has placed me here and my calling to serve others who seek to discover their true self.

These are only a few of very powerful personal and witnessed stories of forgiveness that I have been blessed to encounter. There have been very personal moments of humility in all these moments in my life. Being humbled by the truth of who I was at that time of my life offers a freedom that is new for me and I like it! This was awe-inspiring because I know it is what has allowed me to continue on my *Journey of Intention.*

What is your story of forgiveness? We all have them. I encourage you to go beyond the intellect of forgiving and truly forgive anyone who has hurt you. I understand there are some horrible acts of violence that people live through. I know our justice system sometimes gives us all the permission we need to hate. It feels good...for a while. Does it ever bring us a sense of peace? Not really. Forgive others, do it for yourself. Align yourself with your holy values; it is the most humbling, amazing experience and the greatest gift you will ever give yourself. And accept, truly, accept the forgiveness God has already offered the very moment you were sorry.

Seven

An Offering ... Love

As Jim and I were talking one afternoon; actually he was mostly listening as I was chattering on and on about whatever was bothering me that particular day; he stopped me, and, staring me straight in my eyes said, "I know what your problem is Derlene; you do not love yourself." I was like, "Excuse me?"

"What do you mean, I don't love myself?" I really didn't get it. I was not even sure about what he meant by "I did not love myself?" Is that even a big deal? As long as I was a nice person and good to others, why did I need to spend time on whether or not I liked myself? Ok, love myself. You know that feeling of your heart racing and skin turning red when someone says something and you so badly want to dismiss it and at the same time know there is truth in the statement? That is how I was feeling in that moment.

I asked him what he meant by "I didn't love myself." He explained that I kept using excuses and blaming others to deflect any personal feelings about myself like when I told him the kids really did not engage in meaningful conversation; and Steve just nodding, not really listening; and that my parents only called to make sure I was still alive. "Listen to yourself," Jim said.

As a young mom and teacher, I was asked to speak to a group of parents on the book, *Five Love Languages of Children* by Gary Chapman. While I was reading the book, I took the little quiz that was recommended. It would identify my personal love language. The thought behind this book is that we all receive and give love in different ways; usually one is more distinct in a person than the others. Through this process, I discovered my "love language" is quality time. It turns out, my understanding of what love is depended on how much time I spent with people. It was how I understood that people love me. No wonder when someone canceled on me I would be devastated, or when the kids had better things to do instead of sitting down and talking to me, I would take it personally. This was quite enlightening for me. With my love language being quality time, I can receive gifts, acts of service, words of affirmation, or physical touch and still not understand that I am loved like when someone spends time with me.

Reading this brought me to a new understanding of my "what is love" question I had been carrying around inside of me for so long. So now what to do with this newly gained information? I didn't know. For a fleeting couple of months, I would think about my new-found insight. But then life in the fast lane took over again. Now I knew what it was that I didn't know before but was clueless as to what I was going to do with this information.

All those years before preparing for the talk with parents I had discovered something about how I receive love and now I was being challenged about not loving myself. I knew that discovery was important in my journey, but did it fit into these constant feelings of loneliness, sadness, and self-doubt I was experiencing now on a daily basis?

Understanding that memories hold our greatest opportunity to learn, I decided it was now time to answer the question that I so often asked, "What is love?" My *Journey of Intention* was now calling me to quit asking the "why" question, but to become curious about the experiences I now understood as opportunities to grow. Since I couldn't get past those moments when I felt so alone and confused, there must be some powerful learning that needs to take place so my *Journey* could move forward.

I began thinking about how my life has been a series of people coming and going in and out of it. My dad, serving in the Air Force, would leave and then come back again. My extended family, grandparents, aunts, uncles, and cousins, would all visit a couple of times a year and then be gone again. I never had the same friend for more than two years or so before I was on to a new community to make new friends. I had a marriage to an amazing man and phenomenal father who was always working in and out of town. All of this was beginning to make sense. No wonder I didn't get love; the language I knew it to be was constantly being disrupted. All of this coming and going in my life was not unique or bad or wrong; it was just the way it was. However, for someone who identifies love through quality time, it was hard for me to understand. Even as an adult I struggled with the understanding.

That is where I found myself when Jim made that statement: "You do not love yourself." I did not have a clue what to do next. I just knew this was a life changer for me; time to get really curious! I had been asking Jim and Stacey why, why, why? Stacey asked me why it was so important for me to keep asking why? "Just get curious about it and see where you go," she said.

Stacey suggested I experience Time Line Therapy. At first I was uncomfortable with the idea; what if I didn't like what I remembered, what if I couldn't learn from it, what if.... Oh but living in the "what-ifs!"

I trust her and knew she wanted to help me get past this huge mountain so I could enjoy the benefits of the understanding and learning that it held. Stacey guided me through the process. I listened to her voice and allowed my unconscious mind to follow her words:

I must have been about five or six years old. My dad was leaving to go overseas with his work in the Air Force. I was trying to tell him goodbye and that I loved him but I was crying as a five-year-old would. I was confused as to why my daddy had to go away from our family. He hugged me and he was gone. As I was in that time, I kept trying to get his attention. I could feel the sadness, the fear, the confusion; my daddy was leaving! Why was mom crying? Is he coming back? Why did my daddy have to leave? All the while, I just needed him to spend time with just me. I needed just a couple of minutes to know he was going to come home – and soon. I needed him to tell me he loved me and to squeeze me tight, like he would never let go.

In those moments of the guided state, I can remember trying to figure what it was I was supposed to learn. I could hear Stacey's voice, but I would not come back to the room because I was not sure I had what I needed. I pretty much got hysterical. Finally, after much prodding, my consciousness came back to the room, but I just sat in the moment, tears rolling down my cheeks. I was still trying to figure out what had just occurred and what meaning it had for me.

With Stacey's guidance, I understood what I was to learn from that time of great anxiety, fear and confusion. Only positive in nature. Since my love language was time, I always felt like my dad didn't REALLY love me because he left me and went far away for a long time. What I needed in that moment was my daddy to pick me up, twirl me around, hold me tight, and tell me he loved me! Just dad and me.

That was the mind of a five-year-old child who feels love the most when those that love her are near and sharing their time. I finally got it! The reason my dad was leaving his family was because he *did* love me and my family so much he was willing to travel to the ends of the earth to make sure we were clothed, fed and had adequate shelter. This was *his* way of showing love. It was really difficult for me to write the emotions I felt once I realized the powerful, life-changing moment that had just taken place. I could never get past understanding love in terms of time even after studying the Five Love Languages; it just did not "click." To say the weight of 45 years of confusion was lifted was an understatement!

I now understood so much of myself. My husband always working out of town, my kids growing up and moving away, my parents and siblings not being around for day to day life; it all makes sense why I internalized that as not being loved. Because my husband loves our family, he has always been willing to work hard, long hours to provide for us. (We marry those similarities we find in our father!) Kids move away because they grow up; they didn't move because they didn't love me.

Oh, those moments my family would gather for family reunions; I was so anxious. When my mom and I would talk about extended family I would always say they didn't really like me; they just tolerated me because I was part of their lineage. I always felt like an outsider. I now understand it was because they walked in and out of my life like a revolving door, a problem for a love language of time

I recognize through that experience as a frightened little girl that I am a "tough cookie." I gained a certain independence in my young life. I am a strong, determined woman because that is what I witnessed in my mom all those months while dad was away. Mom loved and cared for her three children, all of whom were under five years old when dad left. It is ironic that I became a mother whose husband works out of town and had to rely on that inner strength and determination I witnessed early in my childhood.

As I began to think about how I was always blaming something or someone for me feeling the way I did, a thought came to my mind: when my family moved to California, I remember saying to a friend, "I have never been by myself before, I hope I like me!" And I laughed. I did not take myself seriously when I said that, or did I? Sometimes the unconscious mind slips out! He looked at me, smiled, and said there was only one way to find out if I like myself or not, and that was about to happen! For the first time in my life, I was going to have a huge amount of time to myself. The kids would be in school and Steve would be working or traveling. That was a lot of time to get to know myself. I was both frightened and curious; did I even know who I was?

That memory of the conversation I had just prior to moving to California came flooding back to me. For the first time in my married life, when I moved to California, I wouldn't have a job, the kids would be in school and my husband would by working out of town. I really didn't know what I was going to do with twenty-four hours in a day; and by myself!

It was one thing to move into a new area when you are a kid and can go to school and get busy with school work and have a place to meet people; another thing to be an adult and move into an unknown area with no outlet to meet others. Since that was what I was telling myself, that is exactly the life I created.

Once school began for the kids, I would take them to school, come home, sit on the couch and have this amazing pity party! I would sit and cry, looking at pictures of my former life, cry some more, check the time, realize it was getting close to picking up the kids, clean up, and leave the house again. This went on for about four or five weeks: poor me, no one would understand my sadness; why would anyone need my friendship; people in California are not like the people back home, they always seemed to be into their *thing* (as opposed to my *thing*?). On and on I would go. It was as if that is where I found my comfort zone – wallowing in my very own self-pity.

For you were in darkness, but now you are light in the Lord. Live as children of light for light produces every kind of goodness and righteousness and truth. Try to learn what is pleasing to the Lord. Ephesians 5:8-10

I was sitting on the couch having another one of the many pity parties I invited myself into, looked around, and thought, "I keep having this pity party but no one is showing up but me!" I prayed that God would give me the strength to get up and go back into the world; to be an active, thriving person once again.

I gathered up what energy I had and went the next day to my daughter's school and began volunteering. My world began to reopen once again. I sure do not miss those private pity parties! I would have my party, and then began berating myself about my behavior. We were so blessed to have a job when the economy had crashed and so many people were out of work; the kids were in good schools; and I got to eventually work at the school my daughter attended. I didn't appreciate all the blessings of that precious time; but that is okay because I understand those experiences are what has brought me to this moment.

What is your story about loving yourself? Have you discovered how you receive love? I invite you to get really curious about those thoughts that hold you back from fully embracing the person of you. Do it! You will discover some truths that will set you free!

Eight

An Offering ... Memories

My curiosity was peaked as I was discovering more about the words and thoughts about myself that I allowed into my mind, and I was excited to discover what else I needed to experience or learn in order for me to step more fully into the person of me.

I began to wake up my inner voice and learn how to use it to put positive thoughts into my mind and use those thoughts to affirm who it is I am. Up to this point in my life, I didn't understand that I could control what I allowed into my unconscious mind. I did not have positive self-talk. To actually change what was already planted in my mind about whom I believed I was became an entirely new understanding for me. I have always known God had this amazing plan for my life, and I was aware I was not thriving like I knew I could. I just did not have the tools to begin to understand how I could shift my thoughts and begin to live the life that I now desired.

I became curious about how I was going to approach this new way of conversing with myself. I wanted to connect with where I went off track and begin to understand what it was I was supposed to learn from these gifted life experiences. Stacey had told me on more than one occasion that memories come back again and again because we have not fully learned the lesson or lessons the memory is trying to teach us. That made a lot of sense. Once I could grab the learning from that memory, a positive learning only, I would be empowered as opposed to being disempowered by the memory or experience. It has to be positive learning that I seek; bathing in the negative does not allow me to grow or move forward for that matter; and I am all about the excitement of a thriving future!

Several conversations took place before I really understood that in every situation or experience, there is something positive to gain. *Every* experience.

After that "aha" moment with Stacey in which I discovered that I was the common denominator, I began to understand the concepts of living in "effect" or at "cause." Living in effect means that I live my life blaming someone or something for the way I think, feel, or react. There was always an excuse for something that happened, it was never my fault. This way, I relieved myself of any personal responsibility for the outcome. It was much easier to blame the way I acted or reacted on someone else, a previous experience, or even a past trauma; whatever may have occurred, it was not my fault. In retrospect, it was like misery was my comfort zone; I knew what to expect, and since that is what I expected, that is what happened. Then, when life didn't "go my way," all I had to do was make an excuse and give myself permission to stay stuck in that dark place in my mind. At least I knew I was alive because I was feeling something regardless if it was good or bad, it was feeling.

When I began to live at cause, that is, not longer making excuses for my behaviors, thoughts, etc., my life became my own. Honestly, it involved being humbled to my knees. It is hard to admit, even to myself, that I mess up or am not living the values that are sacred to me. It is at these times that I have to look myself in the mirror, admit to my imperfection (dang that's hard!), seek what it is I am called to learn, apologize or forgive if necessary, and move forward. Yes, that can be incredibly humbling; however, it can result in an amazing internal transformation, which shows up in my external self as well.

It is remarkable as I look back and see the times I was so disconnected with God's message of love, but in the same breath was teaching others about His unconditional love. I remember thinking, "Well, if I can't be loved at least I can convince others they are loved by God." Even though people would say that God was working through me, I just could not see that myself. I know now that is true; God works through each of us as we learn, grow, take a step back; learn, grow, and take a small step forward. The secret was to become *intentional* when the growth spurts present themselves as a teachable moment; do not underestimate the great opportunity to learn amazing insights about myself which have been offered to me.

I was talking with a friend who was telling me about her parents, most especially a conversation that revolved around her father. She didn't like him; as a matter of fact, pretty much no one liked him. He was not a nice person. We talked about some of her experiences growing up and even into adulthood. None of her memories were positive or happy. She could not recall a time when she felt loved by her father. He never lived up to her idea of what a father should have been. I sat and listened to her as tears formed in her eyes. Her pain was as raw as if she was experiencing her childhood over again.

Our conversation soon shifted to her role as a mother, wife, and grandmother. Her eyes lit up, and she beamed as she bragged about her kids and told of the many travels she and her husband have been experiencing together. Her kids and grandkids are the center of her life. After she shared some wonderful stories of happy childhoods she had provided for her own children as well as the joys of being a grandmother, the conversation turned serious once again. I asked what it was she believed she had learned from her father. Her impulse was

95

to be negative in her reply; her father was mean, uncaring and certainly unloving.

I began to challenge her: there is a positive learning in all this hurt and anger. She looked at me like I was crazy. I just tossed this thought out there: "I wonder how you learned to be a committed, loving mom and grandmother?" We sat in silence as she pondered. I watched her mind look back through the years. She was trying to figure out what good possibly came from her father.

As I began to ask questions, she had one of those "aha" moments. She looked at me and slowly thought through my question. She realized through her father's inability to love her (and everybody else) she knew what love was...and wasn't. "I knew the kind of parent I would be because I witnessed through my dad the parent I would not be."

I repeated what she said back to her and then called her attention to how she described herself as a mom and grandma. She was committed to her family because she knew what it was like to feel that your parent does not love you. "Think about it," I challenged her: "Your father taught you how to be an amazing parent and loving spouse."

"Uh?" her mind was in overdrive. He taught her by his example and she made the choice of the kind of parent you would be when given the gift of her own children. Actually, given the father's life experiences, he was doing the best he could with the tools he had. She, too, had been offered some amazing gifts through his parenting. What she did not realize until that moment, was that she had actually embraced those offerings to guide her as she parented her own children. It is much easier to forgive others when you understand they are doing the best they can with what they know and have previously experienced.

Love is patient, love is kind. It is not jealous, love is not pompous, it is not inflated, it is not rude, it does not seek its own interests, it is not quick-tempered, it does not brood over injury, it does not rejoice over wrongdoing but rejoices with the truth. It bears all things, believes all things, hopes all things, endures all things. Love never fails. So faith, hope, love remain, these three; but the greatest of these is love. ! Corinthians 13:4-7, 13.

I have had instances time and time again when I could not get past a memory or feeling. I continued to work with Stacey and now understood that I had not learned what (positive) lesson my memories were supposed to teach me.

An example of one such memory is from my early school years. My dad was serving in the Air Force, we were living in Mississippi, and I was in the second grade. There had been some kind of uproar about where the military kids were going to go to school. It was arranged that we would go to a private school.

I was playing on the monkey bars with the other kids during recess. The principal came out of the building and was obviously angry. He stomped past us and grabbed a little African-American girl from the see-saw and literally dragged her by her pony tails! I watched in shock as she tried to get her balance while literally being yanked and pulled across the playground. I had no idea what was going on but all these years later I can still remember thinking, "What could someone do so bad to be treated like that?" To this day, I get tears in my eyes thinking about witnessing such horror. I can still hear the cries of that little girl.

This incident occurred in the late nineteen sixties, at a time when our country was transitioning our value system to be more inclusive of all Americans. As chaos and hate surrounded many communities, I was not even aware that people judged others based purely on the color of their skin. It was never a topic in our family. No matter how protected children's lives are, our child world sometimes clashes with the reality of how evil humanity can be at times. This was one of those times for me.

Ever since that time in my young life, when I see racial tensions on the television, witness them in my community, or even hear "jokes" around race, my mind takes me back to second grade. It is at this young age I am quite certain I witnessed humanity at its worst at the expense of a little girl.

Watching the news one evening, this memory was triggered once again. At that moment, I consciously made a decision to get curious and discover what it was I learned from witnessing that hateful, horrible act. I knew somewhere in my unconscious mind I had learned a valuable lesson(s); I now had the tools to satisfy that curiosity. I sat down in a quiet space and asked myself what positive learnings I had taken from that experience. I knew almost at once: compassion and protection of others, most especially children; and power; an unholy power that other people inflict upon another.

As an educator, one of my most powerful teaching experiences was in a class where I wanted to address the obvious power struggle between some of the students. I had not planned the class that day to include this conversation, but the situation had presented itself on its own. The students walked into my classroom and were talking about what was going on between some of their classmates. If teachers pay attention, they can pretty much figure out who carries the power in the class and who the (latest) target might be. In this particular incident, the student with the power was one of the tallest, strongest, and brightest kids in the class. I liked him but I had also seen him use his leadership in ways that destroyed others.

As the students got settled, I turned to the class and announced, "When you walked in today, I got to make a choice." I turned around and wrote the word "power" on two columns on the board. I then invited the students to brainstorm what "power" meant to them. They said words like "money," "Michael Jordan," "the president," "selfish," "getting your way," etc. I went to the other column and above "power," I wrote "holy." I once again invited the students to brainstorm words that meant "holy power." They said words like "Jesus," "the Bible," "kindness," "nice," etc. I listed those words in the "holy" column.

I then turned around and faced the class. I announced that every day they walked into the classroom, I got to make a choice. I could teach with power or holy power. I would let them choose which one I should use based on the words they brainstormed. They, of course, voted for holy power. We talked about what it would look like if I used an unholy power to teach them.

I then explained that each one of them gets to make that very same choice everyday in every situation. Taking it one step further, I walked them into their future where they were in leadership roles at work. They, too, would be in a position one day to make that choice as a leader in their jobs. What would they choose: power or holy power? As the question hung in the air, I watched the expression on the student who held the power in the class; the "light bulb" went on. He got it! He knew he was using his power to destroy in an unholy manner. After class, he came and just said, "Thanks Mrs. Hirtz, I get it."

Those lessons so many years before served me well that day as I was teaching. Having the compassion to love in spite of the behavior I was witnessing, the need to protect the other students, and the clear understanding of the the consequences of using power in an unholy manner, made an impact on young lives that will serve them well in the years ahead. Sometimes I have to control my "mamma bear" instincts to solve all their problems for them. Through story and example, it is much better to bring attention to situations in a non-threatening example so the students can gain tools and embrace their own choices which will serve them well in the future.

That (unholy) power I had witnessed all those years before came back to my consciousness at precisely the right moment! When I reflect on that time as a young child, it is no longer with confusion or pain; it is with a very clear understanding that I am compassionate, will do what is necessary to protect children in my care and am conscious of the effects power has on the powerless. All serve me well in my life as a member of my community both personally and professionally.

I knew I had made great progress when I was out shopping with my daughter one afternoon. A woman, mother of the groom, was shopping for a dress for the wedding. She looked very pretty in the dress but was complaining that she was 5 years younger and 25 pounds lighter when her daughter got married. She was criticizing herself that the dress was too tight, but at least she had a couple of months to diet, she looked old, not youthful, oh those wrinkles, etc. She tried on two dresses, asking us which one we liked better. We offered our opinions. I looked at her friend that was shopping with her and said, "Do you think she knows how beautiful she really is?" Her friend shook her head no. It struck me at that moment how far my journey has taken me. Previously I would have gone right along with her complaining. Yeah, it stinks getting old. Yeah, I'm fatter than five years ago, too. Yeah, I look so old.

Here's the cool thing: It didn't even occur to me to join in the bashing of selves! All I wanted to do was lift her up and help her to realize she is so beautiful right now, at this very time in her life journey! My heart broke for her that she was so distraught.

I was able to be that positive, assuring voice because I no longer look at myself the way I used to. I could name all kinds of attributes that I could have to make me "prettier." It just does not serve me. I now say, "Derlene, you are perfect the way you are today. If tomorrow comes and you want to lose weight, then you can make that choice then. But for now, you are beautiful in the person of you." Truly, it is amazing that I can even type this!

This is how my memories serve me; they teach me valuable lessons which allow me to see life through much truer lenses. All those memories which I have chosen to reflect, learn and change the way I view them has allowed me to experience life within myself and others as well, in a much healthier, life-giving way.

What memories do you have that may be preventing you from moving forward? Are you willing to travel the distance to learn some amazing and wonderful gifts that await you? You may initially feel like it is the most difficult choice you make; however, in the end, it is an amazing life that awaits you! As the saying goes, "What, worth anything, isn't a lot of work?"

Come on! Make that choice! It is YOURS to make!

Nine

An Offering ... Finding Friendship Within

When I initially began writing this book I told Stacey I wanted to write about friendship. She listened, asked a few questions, and let me ramble on. I explained that I have had some really wonderful friends through the years and besides, "Friendships intrigue me," I explained. I continued that I was fascinated by the ways in which girls treated each other, including cliques which were totally new to me when I began high school. It has always been a mystery to me why there are closed groups and people who do not have the slightest interest in getting to know each other. For me, stories of others are intriguing; I learn so much from their experiences and wisdom.

Mostly what I found interesting were best friends: the friends who can finish each other's sentences, stand by each other through the good times and bad, and not judge, just loving you for the way you are, warts and all. Did that really exist? One of my favorite sayings is "a good friend will bail you of jail; a best friend will be sitting beside you talking about what a great time you had the night before!"

Since I moved a lot as a child, I really did not understand the concept of "best friend." I was so glad to have a friend at my new school or neighborhood and by the time we got to know each other it was time to move to my dad's next assignment. I have always embraced this experience as very positive. I make new friends easily and enjoy how we all walk through different doors and yet end up at the same places. It is fun to hear the stories, embrace differences and celebrate our commonalities as well. However, the thought or knowledge of having a life-long, best friend was most intriguing to me.

I was well into my adulthood when I had an experience that helped me understand what friends will do for each other. I had been hurt by someone and reacted in my usual walking away and pretending that it did not bother me. Then I went home and sulked all night, telling myself to get over it.

This particular day, one of the girls I worked with was questioning one of my highest values: my work ethic. I was devastated. One of the gifts I have received from my dad is that hard word is always expected and anything less than 100% just isn't who we are; not in my DNA. I have always prided myself with a job well done. You can appreciate how devastating this was for me.

Later that night, my girlfriend, Cindy, called just to say hello. I could hardly talk because I was still so upset. I kept trying to act like I was okay, but she knew I was really troubled by the sound of my voice. All of a sudden, she said, "I am on my way over." I tried to talk her out of it because she lived about fifteen miles away, it was bedtime for the kids, and we had to work the next day. However, she insisted. I could not believe that she would really come all the way to my house just because I was upset. She was knocking on my door before I knew it.

We talked about the situation, in what context it was said, and how she knew that I always worked hard and did a good job. It was good to have someone else's perspective. We talked a bit longer and Cindy headed home.

After she left, it occurred to me what friends do for each other. I was in awe that she felt like our friendship was important enough that she literally dropped everything, traveled fifteen miles, and came to my side. It was the first time I ever understood that I can let my guard down and be honest about what I was feeling and knew that the other person would not just leave. Previously, I would have ignored my hurt or anger because really, what was going to change? I would still be hurt and I would eventually get over it. Now that I look back, I can see that all I did was run in the opposite direction so that I would not be vulnerable and there could be no more words that would hurt me. "Run" sounded very familiar in my life.

Isn't it true we will walk to the ends of the earth for someone who is in need, but we never like to accept that same kindness on our behalf? Does that make us vulnerable? And if it does, is vulnerability something we want to show? Will vulnerability make us appear weak? My answers to each of these questions were: yes, yes, no, and yes, in that order. I am an independent woman; the last thing I wanted was to appear weak.

"Put on then, as God's chosen ones, holy and beloved, heartfelt compassion, kindness, humility, gentleness, and patience, bearing with one anther and forgiving one another, if one has a grievance against another; as the Lord has forgiven you, so you must also do. An over all these put on love, that is, the bond of perfection." Colossians 3:11-14

When Stacey and I talked the morning in which I announced, "I am the common denominator," I realized the issue was that I cannot understand so much of what is going on inside of me because I am basically not friends with myself. Friends do not beat up each other emotionally, are unforgiving for mistakes, or hold you to an impossible perfect standard that can never be achieved. Jim was right, I didn't love me and Stacey was also right, I am the common denominator! (And all she said was *"hmm."*)

For whatever reasons, throughout my adult life, I had lost – or perhaps have never been – in friendship with myself. To be friends with someone, you must know, accept and love that person. I thought I knew myself but it now was clear I didn't accept me for me. My constant negative self-talk eventually took its toll and I did not even know who I was anymore; if I had ever really known to begin with. I had to really get honest with myself.

As I coached with Stacey, I finally quit asking "why" I had allowed this to happen; not liking who I was or wasn't, making excuses about the way I allowed other people to treat me, etc. I consciously made a decision that I was absolutely done with negative conversations with myself. My new attitude became, "Be who it is you want to be, quit making excuses and start either liking yourself or changing the stuff about you that you don't like." Yeah, a real attitude adjustment! This approach made me very curious and I began catching words that did not belong in my vocabulary that were defeating as opposed to being empowering. As a few months passed, I woke up more and more mornings ready to live a life that was calling me to be more authentically alive. I realized I was now entering into a friendship with myself.

It is like those moments when you meet someone new and want to pursue a friendship. You are curious about the interests, history, and commonalities of that person.

I searched around the internet looking for words or phrases that describe friendship: genuine, no judgment, acceptance, forgiving, dependable, listener, and loves you for you. I decided that I would take a look at these words in relationship to how I currently feel about myself. One of the biggest personal benefits to writing this book resulted in my understanding, forgiving, and loving myself. So let's see:

Genuine - it is my greatest desire that people I meet would describe me as a genuine friend; what you see is the real, authentic me. I am a genuine woman.

No judgment – we all have our past and make poor choices that do not serve us well. Oh the glorious day when I quit judging myself and instead chose to learn and move forward from my mistakes.

Acceptance - favorable approval of me. It took a while, but I am there.

Forgiving - as you know, it took an entire chapter on this one!

Dependable - I know I can count on myself to be the woman God calls me to be; imperfect with a desire (as opposed to a demand) for perfection.

Listener - I now hear what is being said to my body, my heart, and my soul; no longer avoiding, truly present in the now.

Loves you for you - this is the culmination of *Journey of Intention*; falling in love with the human being of Derlene, warts and all.

Although it has taken some time to figure all this out, I am okay with the passing of time. The fact is that I made a conscious choice to dive into the deepest parts of my heart and soul; what I found there was an all-forgiving, loving, and merciful God! A God embracing me every step of this journey. A God who wants me to find courage in my journey. A God encouraging curiosity. A God who said, "Come, wander around My heart, I am sure you will find yourself."

How about you? How does the "friendship" check list look to you? Do you have a best friend who fits the description I mentioned earlier? As you seek friendship within, what would you add to the list that describes you - always positive in nature! Are you interested in wandering around in the heart of God? Where would that journey take you? There's only one way to find out!

Ten

An Offering ... Humility

One afternoon, Sonja was asking me how my book was coming along and I told her I felt like there was something I was still supposed to learn before I finished writing my book; more growth somehow. I did not know the depths of that statement when I said that to her, nor that it would be a chapter on its own.

On January 1, I had officially deemed the year, "Derlene's Year of Health." I made all kinds of doctor appointments: regular MD, mammogram, and dermatologist. I joined a new gym that offered a more intense workout to really challenge myself. One of my personal goals for the year was to ride my bike the 241 miles of the Katy Trail from Clinton, Missouri, to St. Charles, Missouri. It was going to take some training. Okay, a lot of training. Jim had decided he was going to do it as well. Another friend, Nina, jumped on board ready to train and go the distance. It was so exciting to know I was going to reach this huge goal. I had never been quite so ambitious. I was in "go" mode!

I began in early January checking off all of the appointments on my list. My blood pressure was good (check), cholesterol good (check); weight, well, two out of three isn't bad! (I have to have something to work on!)

I went to the hospital for the mammogram just as I had done for years. The nurses were talking about how there was this new 3-D mammogram machine; the latest and greatest. I was tickled and thought how funny that sounded; I cannot even watch a 3-D movie without getting dizzy. Technology is taking us all kinds of places. I left the hospital checking that off my to-do list.

The next day the nurse called and said they wanted to do a more in-depth diagnostic mammogram using that new 3D machine and also an ultrasound. I was a little surprised but joked to my friend at work that those machines are expensive and calling me to come back was one way to get them paid off!

I made the appointment; this time there was a doctor in the room to read the initial reports while I waited. As I was leaving, I was assured all appeared fine. Driving back to work, I said a word of thanks to God for the great gift of technology. I have nothing to worry about and lots of blessings in my life. That bike ride was just around the corner.

As I began my work the next day, I was sitting at my desk and my phone rang. It was the hospital calling once again. Seems another doctor who looked at the latest images was uncomfortable with something she saw. The phone call caught me completely off guard. There was "something" on the tests that made them uncomfortable?

I wanted to say to the nurse, "Hey, wait a minute! I am riding 241 miles on the Katy Trail this summer! Training starts in a month. Really? Seriously? I am the picture of perfect health! I have lots of energy. There is no time on the schedule for a bump (or lump) in the road. I sat for a couple of minutes playing the "what if" game. You may recall, I am an expert at that game.

Coming back to the conversation, the nurse gave me some names and phone numbers of surgeons and said I should call immediately. "Like now." To say I was shocked would be an understatement.

I called the surgeon's office and explained that I could not have the surgery for another two weeks. I was leaving town to celebrate my son's achievement in the Army. I decided that I did not want anyone to know; most especially my parents did not need the worry. (I paid for that decision later!) Steve and I decided the kids did not need to know just yet and there was no way I was going to tell my sister. She is really smart, a nurse herself, and she would ask way too many questions that I did not have answers for. I did not want the questions from her nor did I want to ask the questions of the doctor.

That conversation a couple of weeks ago with Sonja came creeping back into my mind: *I still have lessons to learn.*

We had a wonderful visit and celebration with my son and his wife. Soon enough it was back to the reality of what was waiting for me. Driving to work a couple of days before the surgery, I began to cry. I gave into the fear of having cancer. I gave into the idea that the bike ride just might not happen. That bike ride represented so many areas of growth and potential for me; I had a lot of dreams hinged on that achievement.

I had been only allowing optimistic thoughts and positive results to flow in my mind. All of a sudden, the reality of perhaps it might not be positive results scared me beyond what I could manage by myself. Little miss independent needed to ask for help!

I thought back to a conversation Jim and I had when I first started my *intentional journey*. He was saying that it is okay to ask for help, it's okay to trust people, and sometimes you just have to do that in order to get through the next minute in the day. That does not mean you are weak or cannot be independent.

As I was heading to work to go to our weekly meeting, I could feel the tears well up and start to flow freely down my face, ruining my makeup for the meeting! Argg! NO! No crying, don't be weak. I needed to be strong in this meeting; leaders don't lose it!

I pulled up to the parking lot and knew I would never get past the front door in the state I was in; I called a friend who worked with me and asked for her help. She met me at my office. I sat down and just started crying all over again. I didn't want to have cancer! I have too much to do! I have to ride my bike! We sat and talked – well, really I talked, she listened.

Mary is one of the most compassionate, holy people I know. She offered such kind words, assuring me it was okay to be worried, sad, scared, and a whole litany of other emotions. We talked about how I did not want Steve to see me as weak (why not she asked?); I did not want him to be afraid. In that moment I did not think I would be able to handle having cancer. I told Mary about Steve's family already having some really tough times in his family. Steve had lost a brother at a young age, and both his parents had died because cancer invaded their bodies. All three died way too early, at least according to *our* calendar. I found myself making excuse after excuse about why I did not want to have cancer.

Feeling her compassion and support I gathered myself together. I recovered from my pity party (remember, I am pretty good at throwing those!). The hospital called for some information; it made me late for the meeting. As I walked in, I looked at the Scripture for the day and saw those words: JESUS, HEALER, and LEPER. And there I went again! Waterworks! I shared with the team what was going on. Wow! Vulnerability! Humbling to my knees.

I let go of the fear, reminding myself that God's Divine plan is always greater than my human fear. This was one of those times when I was called to trust and lean on Him. As I walked away from my latest pity party, I realized I still had so many lessons to learn. That moment among my colleagues offered an opening inside of myself that had been off limits for almost everyone in my life save a very few.

One of the people I mostly did not want to appear weak to was Steve. I didn't want him to be afraid or think I couldn't handle whatever was ahead for us. I excused myself saying he already has had some pretty difficult tragedies in his life. Aren't those good excuses? That's exactly what they were. I just was choosing to keep that wall up between us.

Steve kept asking if he should come to the surgeon's appointment with me; I kept telling him no. Then I would get mad at myself because I really did want him to come. I just didn't want to give into what I viewed as weakness. Finally, I relinquished and he came with me. Although I made him sit in the waiting area, I was really glad he was there with me.

The lessons, oh, the lessons. I believe one of the reasons I struggled and kept struggling was because I would not take the time to reflect on what it was I was called to learn. I needed to hand to God what was God's to hold for me. I needed to rely on the strength and courage I always encouraged and pointed out to my friends when they were struggling. I really needed to take my own advice! I had to admit that I did not have control over what was inside my body but what I did have control over was how I reacted. As I lifted up my fear, the word "cancer," and having to (possibly) put a hold on *my* dreams, I finally let it all go. I literally lifted my hands to God and handed it all over. If you have never encountered the profound experience of physically lifting your worries up to God, I encourage you to try it when you are really struggling; it is very powerful. If you have had those moments with God you know what I am talking about.

Surgery was scheduled and I repeated that entire "I got this" process over and over in my mind. Steve was out of town and kept saying he would get back for the surgery. You would think I would learn! I would tell Steve I was fine – no worries. Cindy was going to drive me there and back home. I kept telling Steve this was not a big deal. Perhaps I thought if I told him that enough times, I would believe it myself.

I stopped by and talked to Jim on my way to work that morning. We did some catching up from being out of town, and then I was telling him about my conversations with Steve. He brought to my attention that perhaps my fear was showing up in stubbornness, and more importantly, maybe Steve needed to be there for him as well as for me. It took me a minute to think about what he said. I hadn't thought about Steve's needs; I was so wrapped up in myself. I *guess* Steve could come home if that is what he needs. I could let that happen, I suppose. I was completely avoiding the truth that I really wanted him to come home but just would not admit it; not to Steve and not to myself. I can be so stubborn (a *choice*, I might point out)!

The LORD said to Moses, "I have seen this people, and behold, they are an obstinate people." Exodus 32.9

I am so grateful Steve didn't listen to me, and thankful that he had come home to be with me during the surgery and then bring me home. I had been mentally prepared for a lot of pain and figured I would be sleeping all day for a couple of days; but there was very little pain. After the surgery, we ended up hanging out all weekend. It had been a really long time since that happened, a really long time. Since I was in no mood to stay home and lay on the couch, he was my chauffeur while we ran errands. It was fun.

I did not know what the result would be from my surgery. I had, however, already decided that whatever the outcome was, I knew that I had learned some valuable lessons over the past month including that being vulnerable is okay. I realized how stubborn I could be, that depending on Steve is part of what our relationship is all about, and that I had failed to consider his feelings in all of this. Now I had to decide if I was going to learn and grow from this experience or just let history repeat itself.

Ash Wednesday rolled around and I was asked to lector at church. Once I got there it seemed like there was a mix up about who was going to read the scripture. My friend asked if I would mind letting someone else read. Totally out of character, I told her only if the person reading had prayed and studied the scripture as I had done, would I relinquish my responsibility. I even thought to myself, "Did you just say that?" "Really?" However, I felt like God was really pushing me to bring His message to the children and adults that day. Soon after church was over, I got in my car and prepared to head to work. I did not even get out of the parking lot when my phone rang. It was the doctor calling to tell me the results were back and the mass was benign. She said there was literally a 50/50 chance of the mass being cancer or not. I was doing the happy dance! Thanking God and the doctor in the same breath.

As I drove to work, it immediately came to me that God wanted me to share His message through my voice that morning through Scripture, and then He was going to use the doctor's voice for me to hear His words to me! It still gives me the chills when I think about how everything played out that morning. I am a woman who is very grateful for the gift of ever-evolving technology and a local hospital that invests and uses the best available to serve my community. As grateful as I am, even more importantly I learned through this experience that I need to quit trying to control things I have no control over. I learned that, yes, I am a strong woman; but strength looks different in different situations. As a strong woman, I need to rely on those who love me, most especially my husband.

I became curious why I am so stubborn when it comes to my husband. I came to realize that Steve working out of town had it's positive and negative consequences. Since he has always worked out of town, even before we were married, I have made decisions that most couples usually make together. Sometimes simple choices like what to have for dinner; other times they were bigger decisions like purchasing a vehicle. The time couples spend together dreaming, discussing, and conversing was different for us.

Eventually we had the kids; I wanted Steve to feel confident I was a good mom who could handle all the responsibilities of parenting while he was away. Beyond the day-to-day activities of entertaining the kids, feeding, bathing, etc., I worked, and attended college classes when I could. Since my immediate family lived out of town, I did not "drop the kids off" at grandma's house like my friends sometime did. Plus, I suspect I would not have done that anyway; it would have been a sign of weakness. I never wanted Steve to think I was not capable of taking care of our children while he was away or that I was weak.

I know now this was a survival technique I used to protect myself against loneliness, the fear of making wrong decisions, and sometimes wishing that our life was more like the traditional families we lived around. That independence, sometimes showing itself as stubbornness, served me well when I needed it; however, I no longer needed to be so independent. It was many years later that I realized I had slowly been shutting Steve out of my life. The events leading up to surgery was my wake up call.

I am so thankful for having this humbling experience. As fear-filled as I was at times, I know it taught me many valuable lessons: most of which has allowed me to be more available in my marriage and to know that independence does not correlate with stubbornness. Also, just because sometimes we need help, that in no way means weakness. Humility is one of the most valuable gifts, sometimes given over and over again.

What about you? What is your thankfulness story? Do you need to release your guard and allow someone you love into your life on a deeper level? Are you able to recognize and admit to hard headedness? If you are struggling in a relationship, I encourage you to take a look at your responsibility and accept it, deal with it, grow through it, and celebrate the gifts you have learned. Remember, positive learnings and only about you. Then, you, in turn, will be able to help someone who is struggling. How cool is that!

Eleven

An Offering ... Dreaming

The weeks following my surgery were up and down moments for me. I was so thankful for the negative biopsy, and yet I was having these times of feeling that old nag of darkness. Stacey assured me this is normal as I begin to make new plans and set new goals. Sometimes we just take a step backwards and that's okay. I have realized when those moments occur; I handle them differently than I did years, even months, before. I now automatically become curious why an unhealthy thought crosses my mind. If I need to make a call, I do. I don't let myself stray into the darkness; been there and done that, learned and moved on.

Dreaming and setting goals for myself has been so exciting! When I first started coaching with Stacey, I had a very difficult time expressing any dreams. We spent many weeks getting me to open myself up to possibilities and to talk about dreams. I finally allowed myself to admit that I have an adventuresome spirit! It has been there all along; I am just now allowing it to roam freely in my heart, mind, and soul.

My family tells stories of my great aunt, Maude, who had such a spirit. She would be traveling from one place to another, get to a fork in the road, and decide the other way looked far more interesting; and away she would go. Every time I hear my dad tell the story of my grandfather traveling along a dirt road, stopping to get some gas, only to find Aunt Maude working in the gas station, I laugh and I think to myself, "Yay Aunt Maude, you go girl!" Now when I come to forks in the road, I have every intention of taking the most exciting and interesting path.

A couple of years ago I decided I would take up bike riding. Steve bought me a bike; we should have had a discussion about what my goals were because he purchased a bike that, although very nice, reminded me of something Jessica Fletcher (Murder, She Wrote) would have been riding around town. I had planned on riding trails for miles and miles. My new three speed made it difficult to ride long distances and riding with friends was exhausting! I think I pedaled 3:1 to try and keep up. I soon got a bike that was more accommodating to my goals. My dream was to ride a long bike ride within a year. At that time, I described long as 10-12 miles in a day.

When I found out there was an organized ride for the Katy Trail, I was so excited but knew I had to have someone ride with me; I held on to some fear about riding by myself. We started out as three and registered; eventually one dropped out because of health issues. We trained for months, hundreds and hundreds of miles. I loved every minute of planning where to ride, designing a route that added on miles every week, and pushing ourselves further day after day. Sometimes when I thought I could not rotate those pedals one more time, I would add another mile on just to prove to myself that, in fact, I could. Ten to twelve miles quickly became a distant memory.

Finally, the week came for the 241 mile ride. We would be camping (it was really glamping, we had help!) and riding for five days. It was awesome! We made many new friends, rode some wonderful trails, and completed the journey intact. The last night we stayed in our tent while severe thunderstorms passed over, under, and through us. I would rethink staying in the tent through the storm next time! The next day, the last 30 miles were cancelled because the storm the night before flooded some of the trail.

When Fr. Dan asked me about how it was, I told him about the last day. He said, "Yeah, but it was the journey, that's what it was all about, right?" I looked at him and laughed. "Sure." Actually, I was so disappointed we didn't get to finish as planned that I rode 100 miles the next couple of days to make up for the last day. After that, I decided, "Yeah, it was about the journey, and it was awesome! Let's start planning the next adventure."

Stacey and I talked about all I learned. When I began training, I told her that I could only do this with the support of my friends; training, encouraging one another, and holding each other accountable. Training with them was absolutely essential. I was as much support for them as they were for me. That was one of the lessons I learned: I am a valuable team member. Another significant understanding was I could ride that trail by myself if I had to. I loved riding with my friends, but I realized I have the internal drive and determination to accomplish my dreams and goals without having someone holding me accountable all the time. Finding that out about myself was priceless. I now began dreaming in an unlimited fashion.

One day many months later, Stacey and I were discussing about the time in my life when I could not even name a dream or goal. It seemed so long ago even though I knew it was just about a year prior. I told her that she has helped to open up the flood gates on my creativity and ability to dream and set new goals, sometimes daily! There are so many goals and dreams inside of my heart and mind, I hardly know where to begin.

I realize my dreams always include helping others find their way. I enjoy coaching, asking thought-provoking questions and offering challenges that encourage a deeper level of seeking one's true self; and helping others live their journey with great intention. This is the most wonderful dream of all: staying of service to others, which in turn, allows me to continually seek a deeper understanding of myself. That is the best of both worlds!

"Entrust your works to the lord and your plan will succeed." Proverbs 16:3

Over these past years I realize the most wonderful gift I have received is that I have come into friendship with myself. As difficult as it was for me to talk about some of my experiences, I am thankful I committed to facing those moments of sadness and darkness no matter where it led. Had I not made that choice, I would still be living in a place that made me feel hopeless, sad, and fearful. All of which are disempowering to me and serve no purpose for moving forward.

I was shocked the day I discovered Jim was right; I did not like or love myself. For me, it was the best conversation we have ever had. It was an honest discussion that taught me a lot about friendship. It was also a conversation in which I had to face the truth of who I was allowing myself to become; a woman who was not walking hand in hand with God. In fact, I was using God when it was convenient and suited my purpose; my way, not His. What a blessing that conversation was to me.

And to think I began writing my story because I wanted to write about all the friendships I have experienced in my life, only to discover the most important friendship I needed most: friendship with myself. I do not accept the excuses I have previously made: it will pass, you are just going through a phase, you moved around a lot, too many different schools, and the excuses could continue.

This is what I accept: I am gifted with one and only one life; I would not change any of the experiences I have encountered. How could I wish for that? If I did, I would not be penning this story with the hope that another person would choose to live life *full of intention*! I am answering a call from my God to journey, move forward, there is a new adventure I am to travel. I could not be more excited. I am not going to stay asleep for the rest of my life. If you do not understand what I am talking about, being asleep, just watch people at the airport. The only difference between being asleep in a bed and the asleep I am talking about are eyes are open and bodies are moving – both going through motions of daily grind – certainly not thriving as they live this gift of life. No judgment attached, just observing how many people go through life without intention. Remember my statement that you can only recognize something in someone that has existed in you? I used to be one of the asleep people.

I ask myself this question: what do I want you to learn from my journey? It is my every hope and prayer that as you read about my journey, you, too, will make the decision to become intentional in how you live your life. You will seek to find what is at the heart of that nagging feeling you might be experiencing. You will seek a support team to help you through the difficult moments in your journey and celebrate the victories when you have "aha" moments which you will use to help you move forward. When I look back at the time as a young girl when my dad was gone, I smile. For this memory now serves me well as an understanding of the time in my life that taught me independence. A trait that has served me well thus far.

It is my prayer you understand and accept that we sometimes make decisions or choices that are unhealthy either spiritually, emotionally, or physically; and understand that it is human for that to happen. Do not expect perfection from yourself; you are only setting yourself up for failure. I would encourage you to seek the most excellent you that is possible! In those moments that you feel a cloud of darkness, the secret is to become curious why you made the choice or feel the way you do and seek to change the thought or action. Understand that what you are called to learn is only about you and only positive in nature. I know that you are capable of changing the way you look or view a situation; I have experienced it time and time again over these months. I now seek a life *Full of Intention*!

Dear God,

Thank you for being with me as I continue my *Journey of Intention*! It is with the greatest enthusiasm that I write this letter back to you. Enthusiasm for my future as I stay present in the now of today; enthusiasm for the love that binds my family and friends and all the life adventures that lie ahead for us; and enthusiasm for unmet friends whom I will be given an opportunity to journey alongside as they step into their personal expeditions.

I am amazed and overwhelmed by the constant love You have for me. I feel your love through the amazing people I meet, conversations in which we engage, challenges I am offered, blessings received, prayers to and through You, and celebrations through Your Holy Word. All of these beautiful gifts, from the trials of life to the pure moments of peace, are mine for the taking. Thank you for offering them to me; even though sometimes I accepted kicking and screaming.

My saving grace during the times of the dark journey is that I have always known You were within me; it is only that I refused to seek you out when the darkness dangled its untruths in the forefront of my mind. Even though I ignored You (by the way, I am sorry about that!), You remained constant in Your love for me.

I have heard others say that You have designed every moment in my life. I hear others say, "God does not give you more than you can handle." I do not believe that You *give* me trials or allow situations to occur. As a God of free choice, You do not "cause" circumstances to occur; life happens through choices, either made by someone else or my own choosing.

What I am very clear on is that when life becomes chaotic, a loved one dies, consequences occur for choices made, or some other tragedy enters, I am called to lean on You and find strength in your constant love. I trust that you have my back; I need to use the many gifts You have tucked inside my soul: courage, wisdom, resilience, humility and trust. All You ask is that I turn towards Your Light; You will take care of the rest.

I now realize that when I wrote the chapter about forgiveness that I have missed a very significant point. I have forgiven those whom I feel have hurt me, just as I have been taught to do. I have even commented that there have been times when I forgive only because You tell me too. Today I come to understand that it is not how forgiveness really works. At least it no longer works for me that way. I cannot just go through the motions or words of forgiving if I do not do it with and in love. What a huge burden was lifted when I recognized love in the midst of all the messiness.

So, thank you for continually reminding me of Your love as opportunities to learn and grow present themselves. You are right; it is not easy journeying into new territory, gaining new insights into myself, admitting to my struggles, soul-searching my inadequacies, and all the other adventures I will continue to experience, no doubt. However, I am thankful for each and every one of the opportunities to grow into Your daughter and Your servant, *every one.*

Thank you, God. Such simple words, "thank you." However, I say them in the purest and most loving sense. I will always remember I am made in Your image and likeness; I am sure you will remind me if I do forget! I move forward, making the DASH ever thicker and FULL of INTENTION!

Love ya right back,

~D

Epilogue

I continue on my journey and am committed to remaining intentional in understanding that my life is all about me and the woman I am called to be and to remain in friendship with myself. I understand my gift to myself is to continually learn from every experience that comes along my path. I am devoted to constantly self-checking to make sure my thoughts reflect my actions and my actions reflect my thoughts. I remain steadfast in my love of God and pay attention when opportunities present themselves for emotional or spiritual growth. Sometimes it is as simple as holding a door at the grocery store or buying a coffee for a stranger. Other times, I am blessed to be listening to a young girl just talk about her young life, or partnering with seekers who are searching to become an ever emerging better and better version of themselves. It is my purpose. It is my passion. I thank God for the people in my life: Stacey, Steve, Jim, and Sonja. So many more along my journey and so many that have influenced me and I did not even know it. All of whom have supported and loved me through my darkest moments. It is wonderful to live more fully in the Light! I thank God for the opportunity to share my story.

I can always be reached through my email; I would love for you to share your journey with me or allow me to journey along side with you as you discover and live your true purpose and passion in this amazing journey called life.

You can always email me at derlene@youempoweredservices.com or visit my website at www.youempoweredservices.com, Facebook, and LinkedIn.